THE WAY IT WAS

Stories from
The Grand Traverse Region

Larry Wakefield

Arbutus Press
Traverse City, Michigan

The Way It Was: Stories From The Grand Traverse Region
copyright © 2006 by Larry Wakefield

Photos courtesy of the Grand Traverse Historical Society

Arbutus Press
Traverse City, Michigan
editor@arbutuspress.com
www.Arbutuspress.com

ISBN-13: 978-0-9766104-8-9
ISBN-10:   0-9766104-8-5

Printed in the United States of America

Dedication

ONCE MORE FOR LUCILLE

CONTENTS

BUILDINGS, TALL & SMALL

PARK PLACE HOTEL,
TALLEST BUILDING IN TOWN

For well over a century the Park Place Hotel has been Traverse City's tallest and most familiar landmark. It was built on the southeast corner of State and Park Streets in 1873 by Henry D. Campbell, who named it Campbell House. With the arrival in 1872 of the town's first railroad, the Grand Rapids & Indiana, Campbell thought it was about time that the town had a first-class hotel with all the latest amenities for travelers from the south. The hotel was impressive in those days. It was a wooden building, three stories high, with a two-story observatory, wide verandas for the first and second floors, 50 guest rooms, and a dance hall on the third floor.

In 1879, Hannah, Lay & Company bought the hotel from Campbell as part of a general plan "to make this region in itself the most comfortable and popular resort in the West." Renamed the Park Place Hotel, it was completely refurbished and refitted with gas lighting, large easy beds with springs and hair mattresses, marble-top bureaus and washstands, and carpet throughout.

In 1880, a three-story addition with 60 rooms and parlors was built opposite the hotel on the west side of Park Street, with an enclosed bridge connecting the two buildings. It was called the Annex, and it was open only during the summer. After Perry Hannah's death in 1904, ownership of the hotel passed into the hands of R. Floyd Clinch, son-in-law of Hannah's business partner A. Tracy Lay.

In 1929 Clinch decided the time was ripe to replace the old wooden structure with a new brick half-million dollar nine-story building, with a beacon light that was described by the press as "light of hospitality never fails." Construction began on August 6, 1929, and the "Wonder Hotel", as it was called, was ready for the opening on June 2, 1930. It boasted such modern conveniences as long-distance telephone, hot and cold running water, steam heat, and private baths in many of the rooms.

Declining revenues after World War II found the Park Place in a financial bind and it closed its doors in September 1963. At that time it was owned by five local businessmen who, in December of that year, sold their interests to the Eugene Power family.

Power immediately announced plans to expand the hotel and once again provide first-class, up-to-date accommodations to area visitors. Changes and improvements included remodeling of the beacon tower, automatic elevators, updated telephone, television, radio and sound systems, as well as the Convention Dome, Top of the Park restaurant, and enclosed swimming pool and sauna. Power also negotiated with the City Commission to discontinue Park Street between State and Washington Streets so the new West Wing could replace the old Annex and parking space could be expanded.

The Park Place was purchased from the Power family by local businessman Dan Hitchens in 1981, and later by a succession of individual and corporate owners, including the Traverse City Rotary Club in 1989, and in 1996 by the Regency Hotel Group, based in Sioux Falls, South Dakota.

In 1958, the city commission had passed an ordinance restricting the height of new downtown Traverse City buildings to 125 feet. But in July 1999, threatened by the prospect of an invasion of ugly downtown skyscrapers—and with a deferential nod to the Park Place Hotel's iconic stature—the Commission lowered the maximum height to 100 feet. And the Park Place Hotel stands 113 feet tall, still true to its tradition as the tallest building in town.

CIGAR FACTORIES IN TRAVERSE CITY

It may come as a surprise to many Traverse City people to know that in the late 1880s to the early 1920s one of the busiest industries in town was the manufacture of cigars. Over that period, a total of at least 30 cigar companies were in operation, with more than a half dozen in business at any one time. They ranged in size from factories with as many as 18 employees down to the individual cigar-maker who worked in his own home.

Among the largest companies were A. W. Jahraus, 214 E. Front; R. E. Weaver, 213 E. Front; and Frank Schuter, Union & Sixth Streets. Jahraus had 18 employees, and annual payroll of $12,800, and a production of 25,000 cigars per month. Schuter had 12 employees and a payroll of $3,160. Weaver employed eight and had a payroll of $3,190.

Other good-sized cigar-makers P. A. Clausen, 511 S. Union; Cavis Cigar Company, 114 E. Front; Mert Gagnon, 211 N. Oak; Peter Hormuth, 213 W. 9th Street; A. W. Furtsch, 214 E. Front and Consolidated Cigar Company, 127 Lake Avenue.

Some of the largest companies had their own brand names: Diamond J, Traverse Belle, and Gate Post (Jahraus); Northern Queen and Factory Smoker (Weaver); Pig Tail and Monarch (Clausen). Depending on quality, all of these cigars sold at five or ten cents each.

Cigar making was a labor-intensive industry. All the work was done by hand, and it was tedious. In some shops, to alleviate the monotony, the owner or assistant would read the daily newspaper to his male and female employees while they were working. All the tobacco was shipped in from southern states (one or two local farmers had a go at growing tobacco, but without success) and the local cigars sold very well at every grocery, drugstore, saloon, hotel, and tobacco shop in town.

It was generally assumed that cigar making in Traverse City would last forever. But in 1920, the roof began to fall in. And by 1928 all of Traverse City's cigar factories were out of business.

It was World War I that did them in. Until then cigars and pipes were the smokes of choice with most men (and some women too, but not in public). But the men in the trenches soon found that a pack of cigarettes was a lot easier to carry around than a box or handful of cigars. And from then on, cigarettes became the most popular smoke all over the world.

The same fate befell Traverse City's one and only cigar box factory. The original factory was a small wooden building at 426 8th Street. It was built in 1906 by a man named Corrie Krull, who was killed the following year when the factory steam boiler blew up. The old box factory was torn down when a new factory was built of concrete blocks in 1920 kitty-corner across the street. It went out of business in the late 1920s because by then it had lost all its customers, but the building, occupied by various owners over the years, still stands on the northeast corner of Eighth and Boardman.

THE BLOCKHOUSE

In 1847, Captain Harry Boardman, a prosperous farmer near Chicago, Ill., bought from the U. S. government 200 acres of virgin pine timberland at the foot of Grand Traverse Bay, where Traverse City now stands. In the spring of that year he sent his son Horace there to build a sawmill. Accompanied by two or three hired hands and shipmaster Michael Gay, Horace sailed north from Chicago in his father's sloop, *Lady of the Lake*, and arrived at the site in early June.

After a brief survey of the area, they set about building a dwelling for all hands, including Horace. It was a modest, one-room shelter, 16 feet by 24 feet, built of log timbers hewn square with a broad axe. It had bare earth for a floor and the open sky for a roof and no windows or doors. A kind of open, lean-to shanty against one side of the house served as a temporary kitchen; unlike the house, it had a floor of rough planks.

The log house stood on a grassy flat on the east side of the Boardman River, a short distance from where the river issues from Boardman Lake. Its exact location was the center of what is now Eighth Street, just east of Boardman Avenue.

After helping with the house, Michael Gay was dispatched to the Manitou Islands to pick up another party of employees, who had come north by lake steamer. It included Gay's young wife, then only 15 or 16 years old, and her four-month-old baby; a man named Duncan and his wife, and a hired girl named Van Amburg; and several carpenters.

To accommodate the married couples and the hired girl, a tent made of spare sails was pitched inside the unfinished house. It would remain unfinished until fall, when the mill was in operation and could provide the necessary lumber.

The women got the scare of their lives one day when the men were working on the mill, a mile or so away through the woods, and the women were alone in the log house. Suddenly they heard the pounding of horses' hooves and blood-curdling whoops and hollers. Mrs. Duncan and the hired girl cowered in the tent, but Mrs. Gay summoned enough courage to go outside and face the intruders. It was a party of friendly Indians, who had seen the *Lady of the Lake* sailing down the bay and were curious to know what those crazy white men were up to. Mrs. Gay spoke to them in their own language, a few words of which she had learned while living in Grand Rapids, and they were delighted.

The Indians had brought along some food for trading purposes—fish and maple sugar—and were glad to get whatever was available in return; they were particularly fond of pork. This commerce with the Indians saved the little colony from near starvation that winter.

In later years, the log house was known to the Traverse City villagers as the "old blockhouse." It burned down in 1878.

STEINBERG'S OPERA HOUSE

When Julius Steinberg, an emigrant from Czarist Russia, first came to Traverse City back in 1868, he started his business career as a peddler with a pack on his back, walking the countryside from village to village, house to house, selling needles, thread, buttons, and other household necessities. Though he spoke no English, he soon learned that "please" is a powerful word in any language and used it at every opportunity, saying "Hello, please" and "Goodbye, please" to each of his customers. He was a nice looking, short and compact little man with a beard. In women he aroused a motherly feeling.

After becoming a highly successful merchant in downtown Traverse City, he built an opera house to please his wife, who was musically talented. It was completed in 1894, a handsome, red brick, three-story building on East Front Street. The first floor was occupied by Steinberg's clothing and dry goods store, and the upper stories housed the opera house. It was hailed as the "finest north of Chicago."

Steinberg's staged its grand opening on December 11, 1894, with a first-rate production of "Hamlet." Seats for the performance ranged from 75 cents to $1.50.

During the following years the plays and musicals included such old favorites as "Uncle Tom's Cabin", "East Lynne", "The Candy Girl", and "My Cinderella Girl." Most were good family fare, but one play, presented on March 7, 1905, caused the *Evening Record* to thunder, in high moral dudgeon: "True, it contains a lesson, and virtue triumphs, but virtue dragged the slime and filth of a great city is not attractive."

No doubt the play would seem innocent enough today.

Harold Titus, fruit grower and *Saturday Evening Post* writer, remembered a performance of "Uncle Tom's Cabin", one of Steinberg's perennial favorites: "There were always two big scenes—Little Eva going to heaven, and Lisa crossing the ice. Biggest damn ice cubes you ever saw. With bloodhounds, which were always Great Danes, running across the stage and barking."

Among the famous players who trod the boards at Steinberg's were May Robeson, Eva Tanguay, Mack Sennett, William S. Hart, and Fred Stone.

"Eva Tanguay was shunted in here because of a storm or something and she played two nights," Titus recalls. "She just raised hell around the theater and in town. Hated playing in a town this small. You know, it was beneath her. She just made a jackass of herself."

Steinberg's Opera House entertained Traverse City for about 20 years. But then it began to lose its appeal to the cinema. Steinberg himself in 1916 built a movie theater next door, the Lyric Theatre. The clothing store went out of business in 1923.

The Lyric burned down on January 17, 1923, and again on January 1, 1948, but the Opera House suffered little damage. It took a third fire to finish it. The old Elks Lodge occupied the second floor of the building next door to the east, and when it caught fire on December 12, 1963, Steinberg's suffered irreparable damage and had to be torn down.

CITY OPERA HOUSE PLAY WAS TOO RISQUÉ

T he title, Opera House, is somewhat of a misnomer. In all the years of its existence, the City Opera House staged only one light opera, Gilbert and Sullivan's *The Mikado* which was performed by local talent in May of 1894. Actually, in those days, "opera house" was a euphemism for "theater", which was almost a dirty word in polite society. It had a disreputable connotation, suggesting sin and loose behavior. People who would go to see a risqué play in an opera house, and think nothing of it, wouldn't be caught dead in a theater. Many theaters in those days deserved their reputation.

Unfortunately, the first play at the City Opera House, a melodrama called *Avenged*, was a little too risqué. On Broadway, with well-known actors and actresses, it had enjoyed a run of over fifty nights. But in Traverse City, on Monday, February 8, 1892, three days after the formal opening of the Opera House, it bombed.

A story in the *Grand Traverse Herald* expressed the outrage of the citizens:

> *Avenged, played here on Monday, was the vilest thing ever showed in Traverse City. The proprietors of the City Opera will feel worse than anyone about it. There was a good audience of over 600, and all were pleased with the new Hall, and we believe will not feel disposed to criticize the management, who were as badly "sold" as were the public... The Herald wishes to caution the public of Michigan and the press against the Avenged Co. It is a fraud from beginning to end.*

(Unfortunately, all efforts to find a script of the play have been unsuccessful, but it seems likely that Avenged would hardly raise an eyebrow today.)

TRAVERSE CITY HAD A CANDY FACTORY

Two second generation German-American brothers, John and Anton Straub, made Traverse City a candy making town at the turn of the century. Together with salesman George Amiotte, they started their candy factory as Straub Bros. & Amiotte in two small wooden buildings on East Front Street. A few weeks later however, they contracted with Markham Brickyard to build a brick building, 23 x 85 feet at 400 West Front Street.

Here, with six employees they began to turn out a wide variety of candy at the rate of 3,000 pounds daily. Among the early brands were Viletta Chocolates and Favorite Chips. Also popular were their chocolate-covered marshmallows and marshmallow dates.

The fledgling company grew rapidly and prospered. By 1902 the work force had increased to 41 employees—mostly women who were paid by the piece, averaging about $5.00 a week. In 1905, having outgrown their quarters, they built a much larger factory and warehouse on the northwest corner of Front and Hall streets, and installed the latest and finest in candy making equipment.

Here each week the railroads brought in carloads of cane sugar, glucose and syrup from New Orleans; peanuts, walnuts, pecans and almonds, cases of bon-ton fondants, and tons of chocolate. The company had its own water well and ice-cooled storage warehouse.

It now was producing such nationally known brands as Marie, Mosella, and Violet chocolates, Bermuda Sweets and S.B.A. Sweets. These and other candies were packaged in fancy gift boxes imported from Europe (collector's items now).

The company continued to grow and prosper. It lost some ground in 1918 when, because of World War I, the sugar quota was cut by fifty percent. But in December of that year, when the quota was lifted, the factory worked day and night to fill back orders.

In 1919, the elder Straubs relinquished the reins of management to their sons, Willy and Tony, who did well enough. But in the 1920s, the candy market underwent rapid change from bulk candy to candy bars, and Straub & Amiotte lost out to giant candy making corporations like Hershey and Mars. It folded in 1929, one of the earliest casualties of the Great Depression.

From 1933 to 1947, the Straub & Amiotte building was the home of Burwood Products Company, and of the Fochtman Motor Company form 1950 to 1979. It now houses the North Peak Brewing Company.

TRAVERSE CITY'S POORHOUSE

Back in the days before capitalism acquired a conscience, one of the worst nightmares of poor people was of becoming penniless in their old age and having to go "over the hill to the poorhouse." The prevailing attitude toward poor people was Darwinian: if you were poor, it was your own fault for not working hard enough.

In the early 1900s, Grand Traverse County's poorhouse was one of the worst in the state. A ramshackle old two-story building on Boardman Avenue near the courthouse, it was so bad that in 1905, the county supervisors felt obliged to do something about it—or at least talk about doing something. And as result of their deliberations the county paid $1,200 for 20 acres of river bottom three miles south of town on Cass Road. But then procrastination set in, and it wasn't until 1910 that anything was done.

That year, the state forced their hand by condemning the old poorhouse and demanding prompt action to remedy the situation. In a letter to the county board, the state pulled no punches: "Within the shadow of a beautiful courthouse and in a community boasting and advertising its advantages and resources, Grand Traverse County provides for her unfortunate dependent and infirm in a manner most disgraceful to the county and the state."

The letter goes on: "No provision is made for the separation or classification of the inmates and during the winter months the old people are huddled or packed together in a manner almost inhuman.

In one room with space barely adequate for one person, five

men are crowded, their beds occupying all the floor space. The so-called sick room, 5 by 9 1/2 feet, has room for only one patient."

Stung by this criticism, the county board swung ponderously into action. Plans were made to build a new poorhouse facility on Cass Road near Sabin Dam. A vote was called for and the motion passed, 14 to 4. The new poorhouse was built the following year, 1911.

It was a handsome, red brick, two-story building with a slate roof. It had fifty spacious rooms, all well lighted and ventilated. There were two bathrooms with hot and cold running water. The water was pumped to the building from a spring on the south side of the property.

The river bottom soil was better than average, and in the early days, the poorhouse produced much of its own food. Several acres were planted with beans and other vegetables, and there was a patch of corn for animal fodder. Some of the acreage was already in orchard, and it provided the residents with fresh fruit; in good years there was a surplus for sale. The able-bodied residents hoed the gardens and picked the fruit, no doubt glad to have something to do. They also raised chickens. A resident farmer, John H. Homan, looked after the whole operation.

All in all, it wasn't a bad place to be if you had nowhere else to go. In any case, it was a giant leap from the old poorhouse on courthouse square.

As time went on, the place became less of a poorhouse and more of an infirmary. In 1930, the building was converted into a county-owned medical-care facility and renamed Boardman Valley Hospital. Traverse City physician Fred Swartz was the chief of staff. In essence, the hospital provided long-term medical care, for which there was a great need.

In 1959, the county built a new medical care facility near Munson Hospital, and the Boardman Valley Hospital became obsolete and unnecessary. The building was torn down in 1992.

THE ASYLUM LASTED A CENTURY

Perry Hannah, "Father of Traverse City," was directly responsible for the state's decision to locate the proposed Northern Michigan Asylum in Traverse City. Other towns of similar size were bidding for the site—Big Rapids, Greenville, Reed City, and Cadillac. But Perry Hannah was one of Michigan's most politically powerful men, and what Perry wanted, Perry usually got.

He believed that the hospital would be beneficial to the community, and he was right. For 75 years at least, the hospital played an important role in the city's growth and economy. With an average of more than 1,000 employees on its payroll, it was the city's biggest employer. Over the period of its existence, an estimated 50,000 patients passed through its doors.

Other factors that influenced the decision were the natural beauty of the area, the quality of the land, and, in particular, an artesian well on the site that could supply 4,000 gallons of water a day. Another well, drilled later, would produce 864,000 gallons daily.

Work on the main building was begun in the spring of 1882. An order for 400,000 white bricks tinted yellow was placed with the Markham Brickyard at Greilickville—the same kind that was used to build most of the buildings in downtown Traverse City. For delivery from the brickyard to the building site, a tramway with two-by-four wooden rails was laid down, and the bricks were hauled on special flatcars drawn by mules.

The work was completed in 1885, and the first patients were registered: 43 men and women from the Eastern Michigan Asylum at Pontiac, accompanied by 13 of that institution's personnel, including Dr. James Decker Munson, who became the first superintendent of the Traverse City Asylum.

Dr. Munson, a remarkable man, served longer than any of his successors, from 1885 to 1924. More than anyone else, he shaped the hospital's growth and development. With a combination of character, competence and compassion, he put his mark of excellence on it as one of the finest institutions in the country.

There were no "snake-pit" horror stories here. The patients were treated to the best possible amenities of food, clothing, shelter and entertainment, and the best medical care available at that time.

Dr. Munson believed that a moderate amount of labor to keep the patients busy was good mental health therapy, and by the turn of the century the hospital produced almost all its own food. Under hospital supervision the patients raised and harvested the crops and looked after the livestock. (Unfortunately, as a result of pressure groups in Lansing, the farm operation was discontinued in 1957. It was considered "unfair competition with private enterprise.")

Dr. Munson also believed in beauty as good mental therapy. Over the years he carried out a long range plan for beautifying the hospital grounds. He loved trees. In his travels around the country and abroad he brought back a rich variety of trees to be planted on the land. Among the more unusual kinds are the yellowwoods, pyramidical English oaks, and one of the largest Judas trees (redbud) in the country. Also on the grounds is the world's champion black willow, 313 inches in circumference, and many fine sweet chestnuts, a tree that is almost extinct today.

As a result of new methods of medical treatment and housing, the number of patients dwindled rapidly during the last half of the century, and the Asylum finally closed its doors altogether in 1989.

OVAL WOOD DISH

Oval Wood Dish moved its first plant from Mancelona to Traverse City in 1892. Its namesake product was a thin, shallow, oval-shaped wooden bowl of maple, beech, or birch that became the universal disposable container of its time. Meat markets all across the country used them to dispense ground meat, butter, cottage cheese, lard and catasuet, an early form of margarine. People saved the bowl for lighting fires in the cookstove; they made excellent kindling. The company also manufactured clothespins, rolling pins, butcher blocks, wooden spoons and forks, and tongue depressors and ice cream sticks.

Under the leadership of founder Henry Hull and his son H. Cary, the company grew to become the second largest employer in Traverse City—second only to Hannah, Lay & Company's enterprises. It maintained a work force of 500, plus an additional 150 in the woods, and it had an annual payroll of $200,000—well over a million dollars in today's money.

But then, around 1912, the supply of hardwood began to run out, and the Hulls bought large tracts of timber in the Tupper Lake, New York area and moved there after building a huge plant at the village in 1916. The company took with it at least 100 of its best workers and their families, plunging Traverse City into an economic decline that lasted until World War II.

Oval Wood Dish continued to prosper at Tupper Lake, building branch factories at Potsdam, NY, and Quebec City.

But storm clouds were beginning to gather on the horizon. The explosive growth of plastics in the 1950s—with its cheaper and much easier to manufacture kitchenware—began to dominate the market. The company spent a lot of money in 1958 to modernize its Tupper Lake factory, but to no avail. In 1961 it sold its subsidiary plants at Potsdam and Quebec City. In 1964 it sold 22,000 acres of its dwindling timberlands to Diamond International. That same year it sold its Tupper Lake plant to Adirondack Plywood, and called it a day.

The Hull family left enduring marks on Traverse City. The Hull monument is one of the largest and most ornate in Oakwood cemetery. Henry Hull remained in Traverse City after Oval Wood Dish's move to Tupper Lake, and died here, as did his wife. The two palatial Hull mansions facing each other on Wellington Street were built by Henry (Queen Anne Gothic) and by H. Cary Hull (Classic Greek Revival).

For many years the writer has been in touch with the Hull family in Tupper Lake and Texas. They are amused by the legend linking Oval Wood Dish to Tupperware. No connection, they say, none whatever. Likewise the Florida firm that makes Tupperware, whose chief executive, upon being queried, said he had never heard of Oval Wood Dish nor even of Tupper Lake.

But despite all the evidence to the contrary, the legend will probably continue to grow and flourish for many years to come. Legends die hard.

(For a more complete history of Oval Wood Dish Co., see Larry Wakefield's book *Ernest Hemingway Fished Here*.)

CIVIL WAR MONUMENT

The Civil War monument was a gift from the citizens of Grand Traverse County to the veterans of the Grand Army of the Republic who served their country in the Civil War of 1861-1865. It was dedicated on Memorial Day, May 30, 1890. A crowd of three to four thousand people gathered on the square for the unveiling ceremony; the crowd included 150 Civil War veterans and the sons of veterans, who marched to the town square behind a military brass band.

Mayor Perry Hannah delivered an inspiring address, beseeching his fellow citizens to preserve, protect, and venerate this monument "…for yourselves and your comrades. In a few short years you and I will have taken our place with comrades who have already crossed the river. Let no foul hand mutilate it—for as the works of God are sacred, so will he bless the efforts of his sons, when made in behalf of liberty for the human race."

The 18-foot 6-inch statue of a Union Army Civil War soldier was made by a Chicago foundry. It was cast in zinc metal, then painted white to resemble a marble statue. It is typical of the hundreds of similar statues that stand on courthouse squares all over America, both north and south.

On all four sides of the Traverse City monument are bronze plaques listing famous battles in which Grand Traverse County soldiers participated: Vicksburg, Wilderness, Hatcher's Run; Cold Harbor, Beam's Station, Antietam; Port Hudson, Cedar Mountain, Gettysburg; Winchester, Petersburg, Williamsburg. All of these were major battles except Beam's Station, which most people have never heard of. (It isn't even mentioned in Bruce Catton's or Shelby Foote's Civil War books.) It was a minor engagement between Michigan and Maryland cavalry units in the vicinity of a railroad station south of Petersburg in 1864.

The Traverse City monument was in bad shape. Zinc isn't the most durable of metals to withstand the ravages of wind, rain, sleet, and snow for well over a century. In addition to the damage by weather, the statue had developed an alarming tilt to the southeast, which like the Tower of Pisa, threatened to topple the old soldier over backward. Efforts raised the money for a complete restoration— estimated at $50,000 to $85,000 and the statue was restored in 2005.

The monument stood originally in front of the old courthouse and jail, which were torn down several years ago. It was moved to its present site when the newer courthouse was finished in 1900.

TRAVERSE CITY BREWERIES

Was there ever a brewery in the Traverse City area? Actually there were two: one at Greilickville and one in Traverse City. But only one amounted to much.

In 1862, Godfrey Greilick and his sons built the first steam-powered sawmill in the town they had founded in 1854. That same year they also built a brewery. It stood on what is now called Brewery Creek on present Grandview Road, a short distance west of the old Manistee & Southeastern railroad grade, now the Leelanau Trail to Sutton Bay.

But the Greilicks were lumbermen at heart, and their brewery venture was unsuccessful and short-lived. After a year or so they sold it to John Smith, who in turn sold it to Frank Kratochvil Jr., in 1886.

Kratochvil turned the brewery into a profitable business. He dammed the creek, forming a sizeable lake that came to be known as Brewery Pond, and piped the water down to the brewery to make his beer, which soon became the most popular brew in the area. He also built the Palm Garden, the area's first night club, on Grandview Road next to the brewery.

It was a big two-story building with a wrap around porch. It had a long bar with tables and chairs for the patrons, a dance floor, and two duck pin alleys. It also had an exercise room in the basement where Frank's son Frank, an amateur boxer, worked out with a punching bag and sparring partners. Upstairs there were bedrooms where the patrons, by choice or necessity, could spend the night.

Kratochvil was a big, burly, clean-shaven man who loved animals and kids. He attended the World's Fair in Chicago in 1898 and brought back an Indian pony for his kids, who had great fun riding him and teaching him tricks. One trick they didn't teach him was to pick up a bottle of beer and chug-a-lug its contents. On weekends people came from miles around to witness this phenomenon.

They also came to watch Kratochvil wrestle his bear. The bear was trained to go easy on its master, and the bouts always ended in a draw. Frank had bought the bear from some gypsies. In addition to the bear, he also kept all kinds of animals on the place—deer, raccoons, woodchucks, even skunks. Frank loved animals. He died in 1906, and the brewery and the Palm Garden were torn down soon after.

In 1901, Joseph Gambs, a retired brewmaster from Manistee, built a brewery on East Front Street in Traverse City. Other partners in the $75,000 venture were Ole Bostrum and John Elstrom, owners of the 66 by 232 foot lot on the bay at 719 East Front.

The group was convinced that, despite the vigorous opposition of Traverse City churches and the WTCU, a brewery in Traverse City was just what was needed. Current consumption of beer in the area was twenty carloads a month, all of which was shipped in from Grand Rapids, Chicago and Milwaukee. So why not keep some of that money at home? As a further assurance of success, all the local taverns pledged to stock the local product, which was labeled "Hop-Vin."

Nonetheless, the new industry just couldn't seem to get its act together. Brewmaster Gambs resigned in 1905 and returned to his retirement in Manistee. The brewery got some additional capital from local tavern owner Louis Sleder, Louie's father, but that didn't help much. It went out of business in the middle Nineteen-teens, just in time to avoid a *coup de grace* from Prohibition.

The property was taken over by Northern Creamery and Cold Storage (an icehouse), later by Cherry Growers, Inc., and finally by Northwestern Michigan College.

THE ARMOUR ESTATE

Back in the days when Chicago meat packers were amassing great wealth and social prestige (and on any given day when the wind was right you could smell the stockyards from 20 miles away), J. Ogden Armour, son of the founder, was looking for a place to build a summer home. He wanted a place woodsy and secluded.

In 1919, he and the family spent some time at a small cottage resort, "The Timbers", on Long Lake near Traverse City. It was exactly the kind of place that Ogden had in mind, and he bought it from its owner, lock, stock and barrel.

The deal included 130 heavily wooded acres on the lake, and also Long Lake's largest island, directly opposite "The Timbers."

Armour lost no time in putting his dream hideaway into reality. Cost was no consideration—he was one of the world's richest men. He commissioned a well-known Chicago architect, Arthur Neumyn (who had designed the Loeb family's Castle Farm near Charlevoix) to draw up the plans. A local contractor, Charles Hunt, handled the construction. He began work in mid-October, kept at it all winter, and finished the job in the spring of 1920.

The result was fabulous. Northern Michigan had never seen anything like it. The *Traverse City Record Eagle* called it a castle, but it was more like a palace.

The complex, including the main lodge and the two large guest cottages, had 20 bedrooms, 23 complete baths, 11 fireplaces, and a large living room that could seat 125 people. The main lodge was its centerpiece. It was 250 feet long by 75 feet wide, constructed of big, perfectly matched hemlock logs set in concrete, with a cut-stone foundation and two massive stone chimneys. The lodge was built in two parts separated by a glass-enclosed passageway with a tiled floor.

The main section consisted of a large enclosed porch and an entrance hall and living room—both cathedral ceilings, a spacious dining room, and four bedrooms with separate baths. All were sumptuously furnished with antique furniture and Oriental rugs. Most of the rooms were paneled in painted fir and the floors were of red beech.

The north wing contained a dining room, tower and tower room, dishes pantry, kitchen, refrigeration room, butler's pantry and maids' quarters of seven rooms with three baths and an enclosed porch. All of the main buildings were steam heated.

The service buildings and the caretaker's home all were of similar design. The only exceptions were the farm buildings and the huge boathouse. It was 50 by 30 feet, with two slips 36 feet long and nine feet wide. It also had two dressing rooms with showers and one large locker room with boat and fishing equipment.

The whole complex was beautifully landscaped. It won a prize as the best landscaped property in Michigan in 1942 and 1943.

The Estate was virtually self-sufficient. Its large farm on the property near Fern Lake, managed year around by a professional farmer, produced fruits and vegetables, grains and beans, plus fresh milk, eggs, chickens and beef.

The Armour family and their wealthy Chicago friends didn't mix with the natives. They had little or no contact with Traverse area people. And very few of the locals ever set foot on the property. J. Ogden wanted privacy and that's what he got.

He died in 1927. His wife and daughter Lolita spent the summers at the Estate until 1946, when it was sold to the Gerald Oleson family. In 1978 the property was split up and sold to the present owners. All of the main buildings are still in near mint condition.

MARKHAM'S BRICKYARD

J ames W. Markham left his mark on Traverse City. Literally. The first brickyard in the Traverse region was built in 1866 by Albert Norris, whose family were the first white settlers in Elmwood Township. The Norris brickyard occupied five acres just north of Norrisville between Grand Traverse Bay and Cedar Lake. The high clay bank along the east side of Cedar Lake provided suitable material for making good bricks. Norris Brickyard produced about 200,000 white pressed bricks per year.

But that was small potatoes compared to Markham's operation, which totaled three million bricks in 1883 alone, and employed from 30 to 40 men for nine months of the year. Some of them, the sawyers and teamsters, worked year around, getting out wood for the kilns. It took an average of 2,000 cords of hardwood a year to fire the bricks.

Markham was a professional brick maker. A Canadian by birth, he served an apprenticeship and worked as a journeyman until he was 21, then opened a brickyard of his own in Sanilac County, Michigan. He bought the Norris brickyard in 1874 and completely reorganized and refitted it with the latest in brick-making machinery. His production increased from 5,000 bricks in 1874 to four million in 1900.

Markham turned the clay hill into a gold mine. He opened his brickyard just in time to profit from a boom in the brick market. The first brick building in Traverse City—Frank Brosch's meat market on East Front Street—was built of Markham bricks in 1879. Most of the buildings in downtown Traverse City were built of Markham bricks during the McKinley boom of 1900-1910. The Markham Brickyard got a special boost in 1895, when—after two serious downtown fires— the city council passed an ordinance prohibiting the construction of any more wooden buildings in the downtown area. In ten years Markham changed downtown from wood to brick.

Markham's first big job was the Hannah, Lay Company "Big Store" on the corner of Front and Union. It was built in 1882 of two million white brick dyed yellow. Hard on its heels that same year was an order for three million bricks for the first buildings at Northern Michigan State Hospital, which used millions more during the next 25 years. For delivery, Markham built a wooden-rail tramway around the curve of West Bay and then down Elmwood Street to the hospital grounds. The bricks were hauled on special horse-drawn flatcars.

But the brick business went into a decline after the turn of the century. Concrete block replaced them as the building material of choice, and Markham closed down the brickyard in 1907. It had made him a fortune.

FIRE, FIRE!

SOUTH BOARDMAN WAS CRIPPLED BY FIRE

South Boardman in Kalkaska County, eight miles southwest of the village of Kalkaska, is one of the most pleasant ghost towns in Michigan. A river runs through it—the south branch of the Boardman River—and the town embraces a fifteen- or twenty-acre millpond behind a dam that was built in 1878 to power the first sawmill. South Boardman has something of the charm of an English river village on the Avon or Cam except that there are few large shade trees and no houses or buildings more than a century old.

That's because the great fire of 1921 left the whole town in a heap of smoldering ruins. South Boardman had several major fires before that, but the 1921 fire was the big one from which the town never fully recovered.

The town got started in 1874 when Hamilton Stone of Ovid, Michigan, came up on the Grand Rapids & Indiana Railroad to commence lumbering operations. Stone had been told by a friend that there was a stand of eighty acres of big pine timber near the crossing of the railroad and the south branch of the Boardman River. Stone and several other men arrived there at sundown in the fall of 1874. They proceeded to build a shanty with some lumber they had brought with them, cooked supper at the open end of the shanty, and took turns tending the fire during the night. Two of the men were Orange Row and John D. Dagle.

Stone and his men went on to build a dam in 1877 and a sawmill the following year. The dam provided a fall of ten feet and plenty of power for a muley saw, which was soon replaced by the more efficient circular saw. The mill's capacity was thus increased from 2,000 board feet of lumber per day to 15,000. Stone also built the first hotel, known as the Boardman River House, and the first railroad depot.

The town really began to boom in 1883, when J. L. Quimby of Grand Rapids and M. B. Farrin of Cincinnati built large steam mills there. The population in 1870 was 172; in 1883 it increased to 367. By 1902 the town had four sawmills, a grist mill, two shingle mills, a handle factory, a butterbowl plant, a cement factory, and many other businesses. It also had three lumber camps in the vicinity, a couple of boarding houses, four hotels, four churches, and five saloons. A newspaper, the *Boardman Record*, was established in 1901.

The first big fire took place in 1905, when the Burlson Hotel burned down and was never rebuilt.

In 1911, an entire business block, including a hardware, undertaking parlor, bakery, restaurant, saloon, furniture store, meat market, boarding house, and opera house went up in flames.

The big fire of 1921 started on the roof of Dan Flannigan's Barber Shop and Pool Hall. It burned north through Atkins Hotel and Restaurant, Wakefield's General Store, Brett's Building, J. J. Neihardt's Drugstore, the post office, South Boardman Gleaner's Produce Company, and F. Glendenning's shoe shop, as well as many homes.

And that, for all practical purposes, was the end of South Boardman as a living village.

A brave attempt at resuscitation was made in 1930, when the city fathers filed corporation papers, and South Boardman became the smallest incorporated village in America. Alas, it wasn't for long. The corporation was voted out in 1932.

FIRE AT THE OPERA HOUSE

At seven o'clock in the morning of June 1, 1908, janitor Cash Artlip opened the doors of the Bartak & Wilhelm grocery store on the street level of the City Opera House building. He went downstairs to the basement to draw a gallon of gloss oil (a spirit of varnish) for use in paper hanging. As he stepped up to the barrel he thought he heard a sharp crackling sound like a kitchen match igniting under his feet. Instantly, flames shot up all around him. His hair was singed and his trousers enveloped in flame. The whole basement seemed to be on fire.

Shouting, "Fire, Fire!", Artlip rushed upstairs just in time to meet Tony Bartak's son, Ted, coming in the door with two pie pans he had just purchased at Hannah, Lay Mercantile big store across the street.

"My God!", Artlip cried. "The whole basement is on fire."

Ted used the pie pans to slap out the fire on Artlip's trousers. "It was the only thing I had to work with," he said later.

Meanwhile, Charles Wilhelm was sweeping the sidewalk in front of the store. He saw flames strike the basement window in the areaway below and turned in the alarm.

By 7:30, two fire engines began pumping water from the river at the north Union Street bridge through three hose lines into the basement of the building, which was rapidly turning into a steaming lake of water, burning oil, falling timers, and grocery stock. By this time, the fire was seemingly confined to the grocery store basement, but thick black smoke billowed up filling the basement, the street-level shops, and even the Opera House above.

Charles Wilhelm managed to remove his business records, cash from the safe, and a few other items before being overcome by smoke and led from the store by firemen. It suffered the most damage--$15,000 worth.

From his office above, Dr. William Moon horsed his steel safe to the head of the Opera House stairs and rolled it down, breaking off all its legs. Votruba's harness shop sustained $5,000 worth of damage from water and smoke. Next door however, Cavis Cigar store was unscathed. The only thing removed from there was its pet monkey, Reese, who chattered with profound disapproval at this turn of events.

To the west, Joe's Saloon was flooded, and all of its stock of spirits and cigars was moved across the street. To all those thirsty people who pressed him for liquid refreshment Joe turned a deaf ear, explaining that it was against the law for him to sell or even give it away at that location.

The fire was brought under control by late afternoon. The Opera House, fortunately suffered only smoke damage. There were no fatalities or serious injuries.

BIG FIRE AT SUTTONS BAY

The big fire of 1907 taught Suttons Bay a lesson the hard way. In 1906 the town's only fire fighting equipment was a bucket brigade: a few trained firemen and volunteers passing buckets of water from hand to hand up a line from the bay to the site of the fire. That year, the Suttons Bay citizens voted thumbs down on a proposal to lay water mains with fire hydrants in all the village streets. A year later they had good reason to wish they had voted otherwise.

It happened on a Monday, June 15, 1907, an unusually warm and dry spring day with a strong southeasterly wind. At 6:15 that evening a man sitting on the Park Hotel veranda spotted black smoke rising from the excelsior factory across the street. He alerted employees by crying "Fire! Fire!" and they came streaming out of the old wooden building with flames licking at their heels. No one was hurt, but John Stallman, the factory engineer, lost $80 in the overalls he had hung in the engine room and was unable to retrieve because of the flames.

The old factory, originally a sawmill built by Carr & Fox in the 1870s, was soon engulfed in flames. So also was L. F. Stark's warehouse directly to the north. It had been cleared of potatoes recently, but 150 barrels of lime and $250 worth of stoves were lost. With the southeast wind still blowing hard, the whole town was now in peril.

All able-bodied people in town turned out to battle the blaze. Some 200 men, women and children formed bucket brigades, but not even with the help of a trainload of fire fighters from Northport—who made the 13 mile run in just 17 minutes—were they able to make much headway against the spreading flames.

The wind was against them. It carried sparks and burning embers into the very heart of the village, threatening nearby buildings and houses, including the Park Hotel just across the street. Hope of saving the village was beginning to fade. People began spreading wet blankets on house roofs and carrying prized possessions into the streets.

At 6:30 p.m. Traverse City Fire Chief Thomas Murray received an urgent telephone call from the beleaguered village, pleading for help. He ordered a special train to carry the city's steam pumper and 1,000 feet of hose—along with a company of firemen under John Blacken—to the burning village. It pulled out of the station at 7:20 but, due to an accident in the Grand Rapid & Indiana tracks the day before, it lost some time moving around town on the Manistee & Northeastern rails. At Hatch's Crossing it met with another delay waiting for an M&NE freight to clear the way. It finally pulled into Suttons Bay at 8:20, after covering the ten-mile run in fifteen minutes.

By that time it was all over.

Some people called it a miracle, an answer to their prayers. Just when everything seemed lost, the wind suddenly shifted to the north, and the village was saved.

And the citizens of Suttons Bay had learned their lesson. At a special election they passed a bonding issue by an overwhelming majority, and the water mains and fire hydrants were installed in all the village streets that summer.

THE MAKING AND UNMAKING OF A MYTH

Did Hannah, Lay & Company of Traverse City furnish Chicago with the lumber to rebuild the city after its destruction by the Great Fire of 1871?

Steve Harold, curator of the Manistee Historical Museum, has done considerable research on the Great Fire. His figures show that probably not more than two percent of the lumber needed to rebuild the city came from the Hannah, Lay & Company sawmill in Traverse City.

Chicago in the 1870s was the lumber capital of the country. Vast quantities of lumber passed through Chicago on trains to all points in the west. Most of it was carried there by boat from all the big mills on the Great Lakes: from Traverse City, Manistee, Muskegon, Milwaukee, and Duluth. All of these sources contributed the lumber needed to rebuild Chicago. Traverse City's share was probably one of the smallest. But legends die hard, and this one has had too long a life.

The Great Chicago Fire of October 8-9, 1871, was the most disastrous fire in the history of the nation. Some 17,430 buildings were totally destroyed at a loss of $200 million. Over 300 people died, and 100,000 were left homeless. The fire destroyed one third of the city, covering three and a half square miles. And, if we are to believe another legend, it all started when Mrs. O'Leary's cow kicked over a kerosene lantern as she was milking her.

Nevertheless, there may be some truth to the legend. According to eyewitness accounts, the fire did start in the O'Leary barn. But some observers say that the fire was caused by the spontaneous combustion of a load of wet hay that was stored in the barn on the day before the Great Fire.

In 1871, one billion board feet of lumber was shipped to Chicago. The 1871 production of lumber at the Hannah, Lay mill was 20 million board feet. The total production of all 23 Manistee mills in 1871 was 200 million board feet. Thus Manistee produced 20% of the lumber to rebuild Chicago, Traverse City only two percent.

Incidentally, although the Chicago Fire in terms of property damage was the worst in the country's history (a million dollars worth of greenbacks alone went up in smoke), the fire at Peshtigo, Wisconsin, on October 8, 1871, claimed the most lives. Fifteen hundred people died in the Peshtigo Fire. There were no survivors. That was a bad year for fires in the Midwest, and October 8 was a bad day.

FIRSTS

FIRST AUTO ACCIDENT FATALITY IN T. C.

The first automobile accident is unrecorded, but the first fatality occurred on the night of October 27, 1910. Residents in the vicinity of Fifth and Wadsworth streets were startled that evening about 8:45 to hear a loud crash. Many of them left their houses to investigate. They discovered that a large automobile had run off the end of Fifth Street and turned turtle on the railroad embankment that skirts the Boardman River, at the place 15 feet away.

Dr. E. H. Minor, who happened to be driving by at the time, saw the accident and rushed down the bank to give what aid he could to the occupants of the car. He found Blanche Ramsay, 18, pinned down by the wreck and learned that three other teenagers were underneath the car. They were the driver, Nelson Smith of Elk Rapids, Blanche's sister Clara, and Leslie Wagley.

Dr. Minor shouted for help and a crowd soon gathered. Several of the men were able to turn the car over on its wheels. Except for minor cuts and bruises, Clara and the two young men appeared to be unhurt, but Blanche Ramsay was seriously injured and unconscious. She died at 9:30 the next morning at her home on the corner of Eleventh and Bohemia Street.

Smith had driven a party from Elk Rapids that afternoon to attend a farmers supper at the Traverse City Elks Club that evening. While they were there, Smith took Wagley and the girls for a ride around the city. They started about 8 o'clock, and at a quarter to nine they were driving east too fast on Fifth Street, which was slippery with patches of snow and ice. Smith braked for the turn at the end of the street, but the car skidded, jumped the curb, and flipped over on the railroad tracks, then rolled down the embankment to the water's edge. The car, an Apperson "Jackrabbit" with a cloth top, was demolished.

PETOSKEY'S FIRST AUTOMOBILE

In the spring of 1904 Dr. Oscar L. Ramsdell paid $950 for a new Cadillac touring car. It was the first automobile in Petoskey, Michigan, and it was delivered in a boxcar by the Pere Marquette Railroad.

The Doctor called on the owner of a bicycle shop, Charley Smith, to help him get it out of the boxcar, but Smith declined. So Ramsdell hired two young men, Dan Lovelace and Herman Henkel, to do the job. Lovelace was an apprentice machinist and Henkel a part-time handyman. They found the Cadillac in the boxcar, covered with a tarp, on a railroad siding three blocks from the Doctor's house, and with the aid of planks and lots of muscle, they wrestled it from the boxcar to the ground.

The "great red monster", as some people later called it, looked more like a buggy than an automobile, except that it had a small internal combustion engine instead of a horse. It could seat four people comfortably, five in a pinch. And it probably could out-run a horse but not by much.

Along with the car was a box containing the following items: a jar of Vaseline for filling the grease cups; a can of oil for the transmission and rear axle; an assortment of tools, an oil can and a book of instructions on how to drive the car and maintain it. Dan stayed with the car while Herman went to the Doctor's house to get the horse to pull it to his barn.

There, after studying the instructions for an hour, they filled the radiator with water, put oil in the bearings, and then went downtown to get some naptha, because gasoline wasn't available then anywhere in town. Finally, they attached the license plates—made of sole leather with metal numbers riveted on them, cranked up the motor and took off.

They got to the top of Mitchell Street in low gear, then drove out Kalamazoo Avenue, which was a gravel road back then. Everything was going fine and dandy and they began to enjoy the ride when suddenly the car came to a grinding halt. Dan got out and tried to figure out what was wrong, but to no avail. Finally, he disconnected the drive chain, and they coasted back down the hill to the Blackner Pump Company. There the car was pushed up on a ramp used for repairing wagons, and they found the trouble. They had forgotten to put the oil in the transmission.

Dan and Herman worked all night and part of the next day repairing the damage. Dan made new bushings on a steel lathe to replace the damaged ones, and everything worked perfectly. Then finally they made delivery of the automobile to the Doctor.

Dr. Ramsdell drove it until 1907, when he traded it in on a new two-cylinder Reo from Charley Smith.

TRAVERSE CITY'S FIRST AIRPORT

Traverse City first entered the third dimension on October 17, 1909, when Charles Augustine, a daring and inventive young man, flew his airplane off a hill on the south side of town.

The airplane was a homemade job, a biplane with a fuselage 20 feet long and 4 feet wide but no engine; so Charlie had four of his friends run with the big bird—two at each wing—until it was airborne. The plane dipped down below the brow of the hill, and the crowd feared that Charlie was a goner for sure. But then it started to climb, pretty as a waterbird, and glided to a soft landing 600 feet away. The crowd cheered, photographers took snapshots, and Charlie did it all over again to prove that it was no fluke. It was the first time Traverse City had seen an airplane.

Technically, of course, the plane was a glider. But Charlie announced that an airplane of his design and with a six-cylinder engine was being built for him by W. A. Campbell at the Wells-Higman basket factory. Unfortunately, the records do not show what became of this airplane or of Charlie himself.

In April of 1926, a group of Traverse City businessmen bought 60 acres of farmland on top of Ransom Hill on Rennie Street just south of town for $6,000. They offered to maintain it as an airport for two years. After that, they said, they would sell it to Traverse City or to any civic-minded group, at no profit. The Ransom tract had already been in use as a landing field for about five years, and it was officially registered by the National Aeronautic Association. It consisted of a sod landing strip and a windsock, and that's about all.

The group's plans were shot down two years later, however, when a bond issue of $8,000 enabling the City to buy the tract, was defeated by three votes. Meanwhile, the Ransom site had been declared unsuitable by an airport engineer and consultant, and a commission was appointed by Mayor James T. Milliken to come up with an alternative plan for a city airport.

But the Ransom Airport was still in use in 1930, when a Grand Rapids group established the Jack Burne's Air Service from that city to Harbor Springs. Also known as the Michigan Air Express, it had connections with the Kohler Aviation Corporation of Wisconsin, which had already established an air schedule from Grand Rapids to Milwaukee and other points in Wisconsin.

Scheduled flights to Traverse City began in July of 1930. The plane left Grand Rapids at 10:30 a.m. and arrived in Traverse City at 12:21 p.m., with stops at Big Rapids and Cadillac. The return flight left Traverse City at 2:46 p.m. and arrived in Grand Rapids at 4:37 p.m., after stops at Charlevoix and Petoskey, as well as Cadillac and Big Rapids.

A new airport for Traverse City got started in February of 1935, when a crew of 38 men on a WPA project began clearing 360 acres of city-owned property east of Garfield Avenue, the present airport site. The work was completed in 1936 at a cost of $50,000, and the Ransom field was officially closed.

Penn Central Airplanes opened a regularly scheduled air passenger serviced in July of 1938, and a huge crowd was on hand to greet the first arrival. Its equipment consisted of two Boeing 247-Ds with a capacity of 10 passengers, a pilot and copilot; its top speed was 200 mph. Another milestone was passed on July 20 when Penn Central carried the first airmail from Traverse City. Postmaster Jerome Wilhelm announced that over 3,000 letters went out.

Following Penn Central, Traverse City has been served in succession by Capitol Airline, North Central Airline, Republic Airlines, Northwest Airline, and several regional airlines.

Passenger volume has increased from 4,818 in 1948 to 398,268 in 2000.

THE FIRST CHERRY TREES

Who planted the first cherry trees in the Grand Traverse region?

It may have been a tie—or something very close to it— between two Indian missionaries, Rev. Peter Dougherty and Rev. George H. Smith. The two men were good friends and consulted frequently on even such mundane matters as horticulture.

Dougherty found huge apple trees growing at Old Mission in 1837; they had been planted by the Indians. He planted more apples and other fruit trees, including pears, plums, and peaches— but no cherries. That was because his Indian agricultural teacher, John Johnstone, warned him that cherries would not do well this far north—a bad call if there ever was one. Later, however, Dougherty set out several cherry trees in his orchard at New Mission at Omena, where he moved his flock in 1852. (Omena was named by the Indians for one of Dougherty's favorite expressions, which amused them; Omena is an Indian word meaning "Is it so?")

About the same time, his fellow missionary George N. Smith was planting a large orchard, including cherry trees, at his mission settlement at Northport. By the 1870s, almost every farm family in the region had at least a few cherry trees for their own use. One of the first cherry orchards of any size was Ridgewood Farm near the tip of Old Mission Peninsula. It was planted in 1893 for owner O. H. Ellis by John Kroupa, who set the trees 20 feet apart. Other early cherry growers on the peninsula were D. H. McMullen, Arthur McManus, Oliver Lardie, Guy and William Thomkins, George Jameson, and the five Carroll brothers—Arthur, Will, Stephen, Lawrence, and Alex, all neighbors. By the 1890s, large quantities of cherries were being shipped to market by boat.

Birney J. Morgan is mistakenly credited with having planted the first commercial cherry orchard in the region. But he was preceded many years earlier by the peninsula farmers already mentioned and others. Around 1900 Morgan bought 110 hilly acres just west of what is now Tom's Shopping Center on M-72 at the intersection with M-22 on West Bay, and planted a fruit orchard—but only 10 acres were in cherries. A year or two earlier, James W. Markham, of brickyard fame, planted a large cherry orchard near Greilickville. Other early orchardists were W. B. Miller of Glen Arbor; Fred Baumberger, Steiner Garthe, the Scott brothers, Wilbur Steele, M. O. Morgan and Byron Woolsey, at Northport; A. J. "Gus" Rogers at Empire; and Dr. C. J. Kneeland in the hills west of Traverse City near Hickory Hills ski slopes.

By 1914, cherries had surpassed apples in market value. On August 20 of that year, the *Traverse City Record Eagle* ran a banner headline: "HALF MILLION DOLLAR CHERRY CROP." It also reported that 240 railroad car loads had been shipped out from Traverse City to markets in Detroit and Chicago.

The first cherry cannery in the area was built in 1902 by a consortium of Birney Morgan, Perry Hannah, and Dr. Kneeland. It was on Hall Street in the building later occupied by Red Mill Lumber Company. It was called the Traverse City Canning Company.

THE FIRST WHITE MEN

The first white men to enter the Grand Traverse region were the *coureurs de bois*, unlicensed traders and trappers who left the settlements at Quebec and Montreal and lived in the woods with the Indians. (All traders were required to be licensed; but licenses were granted only to a favored few.)

The most famous among them was Etienne Brule, chief lieutenant of early explorer Samuel de Champlain, who sent Brule into the wilderness in 1610 to learn about the Indians and the "big inland water." Brule lived among the Hurons and other tribes and probably saw all the Great Lakes. He was finally killed in a quarrel with the Indians and his remains were cannibalized—or so the story goes.

The *coureurs de bois* (literally "runners of the woods" in French) were followed by more or less official explorers like Joliet and LaSalle, who were still looking for a passage to the Indies, and by the black-robed Jesuit priests, who yearned to Christianize the heathen. Fathers Dablon and Allouez established a mission and trading post at Mackinac around 1670 and another at Green Bay a year or two later. Father Marquette, returning in 1674 from a canoe voyage of exploration on the Mississippi River, died somewhere on the northeast shore of Lake Michigan—perhaps at the mouth of the Betsie River at Frankfort or at Ludington, both communities claim the distinction.

Dr. M. L. Leach in his *History of the Grand Traverse Region* (Traverse City 1883) tells an interesting story about a possible very early white settler in the region. Leach's friend James J. McLaughlin of Elk Rapids told him that in 1855 he came across the remains of a log cabin on Elk Lake about four rods south of the Grand Traverse/ Antrim county line. It had been built of cedar logs, and there was a stone fireplace in one corner. Nothing remained of the roof and the logs had rotted to the ground. McLaughlin concluded that it must have been built by a white man at least a generation or two earlier— since the Indians never built that kind of habitation. It seems likely that the cabin was the work of a French-Canadian trapper or trader.

Of all the early European explorers and colonists who came in contact with the native Americans, the French were by far the most kindly and understanding. They liked and respected the Indians and often took Indian women as wives. It was, of course, to their advantage to get along with the Indians, since they were after furs—beaver, mink, fox and otter—which brought fabulous prices in Europe. For the same reason, they discouraged colonization, since it would interfere with the fur trade.

The British used the Indians but regarded them with disdain. It remained for the brutal, gold-crazed Spaniards to slaughter hundreds of thousands of Indians in Latin America in the name of the Blessed Lamb.

TRAVERSE CITY'S FIRST CEMETERY

Where did the early Traverse City settlers bury their dead? The early settlers were mostly young people (Perry Hannah himself was only 27 when he started the settlement in 1851) and death in the first few years was a rare event. The first occurred in the winter of 1852-53, when a young man was killed accidentally at the first lumber camp on the Boardman River. Early in the following summer another young man was taken sick at the company boarding house on South Union Street. Under the supervision of Tracy Lay, Hannah's partner, the sick young man was kindly cared for in comfortable quarters at the old boarding house near the old mill on Mill Creek, and attended by young Dr. Goodale, who worked for Hannah, Lay & Company, but was available to all who needed his services.

Later that year, a schooner carrying a destitute family named Churchill docked at the settlement. Mrs. Churchill, desperately ill, was taken ashore and placed in the care of Dr. Goodale and volunteer nurses, but lived only a few days.

According to early historian Dr. M. L. Leach, "All three were buried on the sandy plain, not far from the margin of the bay." (The sandy plain was probably on the west side of town in the vicinity of North Division Street.) Dr. Leach wrote that, as the years went by, "a thriving village has extended its streets and buildings above the forgotten graves, all traces of which have long since disappeared."

Shortly after these deaths, a small public cemetery was established on the Boardman River in what is now Hannah Park, where the old Carnegie Library on Sixth Street stands today, across the street from the historic Perry Hannah house. This served its purpose until 1863, when Hannah donated 40 acres to the city for Oakwood Cemetery. It was opened on September 27, 1863, and the comparatively few remains at the old burying ground were transferred to the new one soon thereafter.

The story goes that it was Mrs. Perry Hannah who was responsible for the transfer. She didn't like the idea of having a cemetery across the street from their palatial new home, and persuaded her husband to establish Oakland Cemetery. It's an amusing story but it can't be true because Hannah didn't finish the new house until 1894. The first house on Sixth Street was built in 1885 by Hannah's lumberyard foreman at the mill, Cuyler Germaine. He died the following year.

FIRST AIRPLANE FLIGHT

On the first day of December, 1911, an estimated 5,000 Traverse City area people turned out to witness a real airplane in operation for the first time.

Two aviators from Chicago, pilot Vandie Ludwig and his mechanic F. W. H. Gren, arrived in Traverse City by train on Saturday night, November 26, and prepared to perform three days of flying exhibitions over the city in their two-seater Curtis biplane. Ludwig, a noted flyer, had been putting on such exhibitions around the country for the past two years.

The plane itself had arrived in crates by railroad express that morning, and was unloaded at the Traverse City Iron Works. The two men spent most of the day on Sunday, putting the craft together. The first exhibition was scheduled for Monday afternoon.

Meanwhile, Ludwig inspected two possible sites for the event—the Fairgrounds and the 12th Street grounds—and decided that the latter would be the best for takeoff and landing. It was planned to set up an enclosure there and a big Chautauqua tent to which all 25-cent ticket-holders would be admitted. The Traverse City Board of Trade (predecessor of the Chamber of Commerce) had been busy for a week or more, promoting the event and selling tickets.

On Sunday afternoon, the assembled plane was taken to the 12th Street grounds, so as to have everything ready for the flight on Monday afternoon. But an early morning snow and sleet storm, with winds up to 65 miles per hour, made the afternoon flight impossible, and the plane was returned to the Iron Works. The high winds also made it impossible to erect the big tent, so the exhibition was postponed until Tuesday afternoon, weather permitting. Ludwig and Green promised to stay in town until the weather was favorable.

But the weather was bad for the next two days, and it wasn't until Friday morning that the first flight was made. Although the wind was strong and the crowd of spectators surged all over the field, Ludwig was determined to give them their money's worth with at least one exhibition flight.

The plane rose to a height of about 200 feet, circled the grounds twice, and then sailed over the Asylum grounds. Upon his return, however, Ludwig flew only a small part of the field and made a short landing. Unfortunately, the rear wheel ran over a stump and its tire was punctured. In addition, one of the connecting rods in the fuselage was broken in the landing, making it impossible to conduct another exhibition flight until the damage was repaired.

Ludwig explained that the crowd was so great that he couldn't pick out a suitable landing place without danger of injuring several people. He said he was sorry he couldn't spend any more time in Traverse City and hoped that the people would understand.

Needless to say, the people were bitterly disappointed.

THE FIRST CHERRY FESTIVAL

The first Cherry Festival in 1928 was preceded by two Blessing of the Blossom festivals in 1925 and 1926.

For many years previously, a brief religious ceremony called the Blessing of the Blossoms was conducted yearly by a member of the clergy and his acolytes. The ceremony took place in May when the cherry trees were in full bloom. Its purpose was to invoke the deity's intercession for a bountiful harvest. It has a long tradition, dating back to the beginnings of agriculture, and it continued to this day.

The first Blossom Festival was held on Friday, May 22, 1925, and it was a miniature Cherry Festival. It was organized by Jay P. Smith, editor of the *Traverse City Record Eagle*, and Harold Titus, orchardist and writer. It had a queen and her court, a "mile-long" parade, and many other activities. The big differences between it and the Cherry Festivals was that it all happened in a single day, that it took place in blossom time instead of harvest time, and that Queen Gertrude Brown was chosen by drawing names from a hat.

The second Blossom Festival, held on May 28, 1926, was almost a carbon copy of the first—except that Queen Charlotte Kearns was selected by popular ballot.

The first Michigan Cherry Festival was scheduled for 1927, but had to be cancelled because a late frost seriously damaged the crop. It was held on July 19, 1928, and took place in one day. Queen Helen Boughey was crowned by Michigan Governor Fred W. Green. The Prince and Princess were Dick Bryant and Peggy Beers.

In 1929 the festival was expanded to two days, July 18 and 19, and another day was added in the 2nd festival in 1930, which was packed by an estimated 100,000 people. The Michigan Legislature passed a resolution making the Cherry Festival a national celebration.

The National Cherry Festival continued with three-day celebrations until 1942. Because of World War II, no festivals were held from 1941 to 1947. In 1941, a controversy arose over the selection of Senorita Christine Michels as Cherry Festival Queen—she was the daughter of the Chilean ambassador. The *Lansing Journal* grumbled that the choice was "ill-advised", but Queen Christine won the hearts of all her subjects with her beauty and charm. Nevertheless, the festival board quickly passed a resolution limiting the choice of Queen to Michigan girls only. (U. S. Senator Arthur Vandenberg was a good friend of the Chilean ambassador, and some people believed he had used his influence in the choice.)

After a hiatus of seven years, the festival was resumed with a two-day schedule in 1948 and 1949. It was again increased to three days from 1950 to 1961 inclusive, when it was reduced to two days, 1962 and 1963. In 1964 it was expanded to five days and later to seven days.

By far the largest crowd ever to attend a Cherry Festival was in 1975, when President Gerald Ford and Betty Ford led the Grand Royale Parade. U. S. Secret Service agents estimated the crowd at 300,000, an all-time record.

FIRST GASOLINE STATION

Where was the first gasoline filling station in Traverse City? Right where it is now, at the northwest corner of State and Union Streets. Right where it has always been since Charles E. Rennie, owner of Rennie Oil Company and dealer for Napoleon Cars and Trucks, established it in 1919.

In 1918 Rennie was granted permission by the city to install a gasoline filling station on the Union Street side of their car store. The storage tanks were buried and the filling station erected in the spring of 1919.

Henceforth it became known as the "Pioneer Station of the North" and its proud boast was "the largest and most complete gasoline filling station north of Grand Rapids." It also offered tires at discounted prices, auto repairs, oil change and lubrication service. One of its specialized services was a fleet of two air-compression trucks operating 24 hours a day to help motorists stranded by a flat tire. Most early auto drivers could pull a wheel and patch a punctured inner tube. But even though most of them carried an air pump, it was a daunting and arduous task to inflate a tire by hand.

Charles E. Rennie was the son of John "Black Jack" Rennie, one of Traverse City's most colorful characters. After bossing Perry Hannah's logging operations for several years, he became the city's Chief of Police in 1894 and also its Fire Chief in 1897. A big, powerful, but congenial sort of man with an easy air of authority, he struck fear in the hearts of petty thieves and shysters, whom he escorted to the city limits astride his horse Dogwood and whose speedy departure he hastened with a crack of his blacksnake whip. The Rennies were among the most highly respected of the early pioneer families.

Tragedy struck the family on June 22, 1933, when 27-year-old Charles, Jr., who had joined his father as Vice-president of the Rennie Oil Company, was lost in an airplane crash on Lake Michigan. Also lost were his friend James Gillette, owner and pilot of the pontoon plane, and Peter Keller, mechanic. The only survivor was Rennie's wife Margaret, who was spotted lying on a makeshift raft by a carferry captain and rescued after her 34 hour ordeal on the open water.

Thirty-two years later, a cruel twist of fate struck the family another blow.

On April 13, 1965, Ferris J. "Pete" Rennie (Charles Jr.'s brother) disappeared on West Grand Traverse Bay while heading for ice-bound Marion Island on his air-propelled amphibious sled. A Coast Guard helicopter, sent to investigate, found the sled floating in a small pool of open water, but no trace of Pete. A later investigation concluded that he had left the sled because of engine trouble and was picking his way to the island on foot over rotten ice when he fell through it and drowned. In any case, he was never seen or heard from again, and his body was never recovered.

Pete's purpose in visiting the island that morning was to carry supplies to island caretaker Ralph Matthews and his wife. The company had acquired ownership of the island in the early 1950s, and it became Pete's favorite project to develop it as a wilderness park, with picnic and camping facilities, a large boat dock, nature trails and wildlife refuge, all open to the public.

The Pioneer Station of the North is still doing business at the same old stand, but some changes have taken place over the years.

In 1951, the old building was torn down and a new one constructed.

In 1971, Clint Kinney, its oldest employee, who had operated the station for a quarter century, bought it from the Rennie company; and the sign now reads "Kinney's Pioneer Service."

In 1985, Clint Kinney retired and sold the business to his son Lon. That same year, the gas pumps were removed, and the company focused its attention on auto repairs and maintenance service. Selling gas wasn't profitable enough, Lon says. They needed the space for parking.

Rennie's storage tank farm and marine terminal at Greilickville was established in the mid 1930s. It is now owned by the Marathon Oil Company and the big tankers are still a familiar sight, unloading their cargoes of gas and oil.

TRAVERSE CITY'S FIRST SCHOOL

Traverse City's first public school opened in the spring of 1853. The schoolhouse was a dilapidated and abandoned log cabin. It was built by lumberman John B. Spencer, and used by him as a stable for horses or oxen while skidding out sawlogs from the woods in the winter of 1851-52.

Under the supervision of Albert Tracy Lay, the building was repaired and furnished with such school equipment as was available, all at the expense of Hannah, Lay & Company. It stood on the still-wild-blueberry-bush-covered outskirts of town, at some distance east of the village. Its exact location is lot 3 of block 2 on the south side of Front Street, a short distance east of Boardman Avenue.

It had a door on the west side and two small windows, one near the door and the other on the east side. A big wood-burning stove stood in the middle of the room. The teacher's desk was near the door, and a blackboard hung against the wall nearby. The desks were neatly made but unpainted. The floorboards were bare and the cracks between them in some places were wide enough for a small snake to squeeze through. This happened on at least one occasion, causing the teacher and the girls to climb up on their seats for safety until the boys were able to evict the intruder.

The schoolmarm was fifteen-year-old Helen Goodale. She was the daughter of Dr. David C. Goodale, who had come with his family from Vermont in 1853, to manage the Hannah, Lay boarding house. It was part of his contract with the company that eldest daughter Helen should teach school. Her starting salary was $1 per week and board, and the company promised to make up any deficit if the people failed to pay the full amount. Helen lived with her family at the boarding house while teaching reading, spelling, arithmetic, and geography at the school.

Her first class numbered eleven children of ages six to sixteen; Albert Norris was the oldest—a year older than the teacher. In the following term, enrollment increased to seventeen pupils.

Helen had a long walk from the boarding house to the school. On the direct route past the sawmill there was no bridge across the river except a narrow board footpath on the boom of logs near the mill. It was considered not very safe or pleasant for a woman to cross, but the men at the mill, with respectful gallantry, were always glad to lead the schoolmarm across.

At the end of her first term of school Helen went to Chicago for further study. She returned to the log schoolhouse the next spring, and was given a raise to 50 cents per day. A few years later she married Thomas A. Hitchcock.

FIRST ALL WHITE SCHOOL

The first white school in the Traverse region had only five pupils, all of whom were a few years older than their teacher, Stephen E. Wait, who was nineteen. Their classroom was the cabin of the schooner *Madeline*, and the ship also served as their living quarters during the winter of 1851-52.

In the fall of 1851, the *Madeline* put in at Old Mission harbor with the intention of wintering somewhere in the vicinity. The five members of its crew were William Bryce, the Fitzgerald brothers—William, Michael, and John—and a cook named Edward Chambers. All were able seamen. Two of them had been masters of their ships during the previous season, but none had any formal schooling and were barely able to read and write. They were eager nevertheless to remedy that deficiency, and they hired young Wait to tutor them. His salary was $20 per month from each of them except the cook, who paid with his services. Stephen Wait previously had been teacher at the Indian school at Old Mission.

All of them agreed that rather than stay at Old Mission for the winter, they should find a more suitable place without interruption and other distractions. So they chose the snug uninhabited Bowers Harbor on the opposite (west) side of Old Mission peninsula, moved the *Madeline* around to that place, and anchored her securely in its calm waters for the winter. From the start they conformed to a regular schedule of study hours and submitted cheerfully to a strict school discipline.

After school hours, they got plenty of exercise cutting firewood which they carried to the ship in its yawl and, after the lake froze, over the ice. It is said that they also indulged in snowball fights with the enthusiasm of normal schoolboys. Except for an occasional visit to Old Mission before the snow got too deep, they were completely cut off from the outside world. But the experience turned out well in every respect.

Afterward, at least four of the men went on to long and successful careers on the Great Lakes: the Fitzgeralds as well-known ship captains, and cook Edward Chambers as a veteran lighthouse keeper; unfortunately, William Bryce was somehow lost track of. John Fitzgerald was the grandfather of Edmund Fitzgerald, whose ill-fated namesake went down wilh all hands in the great storm of November 10, 1975, on Lake Superior.

Stephen Wait was one of Traverse City's earliest pioneers, and he had a long, productive, and interesting life. Born in Vermont, he came to Old Mission with his parents in the summer of 1850. Wait—a good carpenter as well as school teacher—worked for Hannah, Lay & Company helping to build its boarding house; and in 1856 he worked for Dexter & Noble at Elk Rapids as a carpenter and joiner. During this time he planned and supervised the building of the *Albatross,* the first boat of its kind to navigate the inland Chain of Lakes.

From 1866 to 1871 Wait was a clerk in Hannah, Lay's company store, and in the spring of 1871 he took a position as clerk and steward on the company's new propeller, *City of Traverse.*

In 1872 Wait started work at L. W. Hubbard's drugstore on East Front Street as cashier and bookkeeper, and four years later he purchased the business. He and his two sons, Edmund and Cyrus, formed a partnership in 1901 and moved the drugstore to the new Masonic Building on Front and Union, where they did business at Wait's Pioneer Drugs until he died in 1919.

Wait, a thoroughly nice guy, was an enthusiastic and talented amateur photographer, and Traverse City is indebted to him for the many excellent photographs he took of the city and the area during his lifetime. He was a perfect rebuttal to the cynical old adage that nice guys finish last.

THE INDIANS WERE HERE FIRST

Indians were the first Americans. Archeologists disagree about when they came, but not at all whence and how. The primitive people who populated the Americas crossed from Siberia to Alaska on a "land bridge" possibly as long as 50,000 years ago, possibly earlier. At periods of time during the ice ages, the glaciers locked up so much water that Siberia and Alaska were joined by a wide "land bridge" as wide as the State of Texas.

In small family groups or tribes these nomadic hunters wandered into the Americas over a very long period of time. It was not so much a migration as a slow drift of hunting people following the game. (One anthropologist has estimated that if they moved on an average of only five miles a year, there would have been time for them to penetrate the continents from the Pacific to Atlantic oceans and south to the tip of Patagonia.)

It is important to remember that these primitive stone-age people were of the genus "homo sapiens" even as you and I. They were in no way inferior intellectually or physically. They had the capacity to produce—a few thousand years after their arrival—the great civilizations of Mexico and Peru, cultures that in some ways rivaled Western Christendom during the Renaissance. They devised a more accurate calendar than ours, for example, and discovered the concept of zero before the Arabs.

The roving Paleo-Indians reached Michigan and the Grand Traverse region probably 10,000 years ago, as the glaciers retreated. They left their calling cards: the exquisitely fashioned bifacially-fluted Clovis projectile points—named after an archeological site in New Mexico. They have been found all over Michigan, along with the remains of one of the big animals they hunted, the mastodon. The Clovis points were spearheads launched by a throwing stick or atlati; the bow-and-arrow was invented much later.

The native Americans whom the first French explorers encountered in northern Michigan were the Chippewas and the Ottawas. Both were of Algonquin stock, along with their brothers, the Potawatomies; and they were friendly with the Hurons, who, though of Iroquoian lineage, were being decimated by the Iroquois, the fiercest, bravest and cruelest of all the Eastern Woodland Indians. This is not to say that the Chippewas were without valor; they, in turn, had driven the formidable Santee Sioux from western upper Michigan.

In the Michigan Indians were a semi-sedentary people. They subsisted by hunting, fishing, gathering, and rudimentary farming; in small gardens they raised corn, squash, and other vegetables. For clothing they used the furs and skins of wild animals, and they lived in bark-covered hogans and teepees. They had a complex social organization and strong family ties. For the most part, they were friendly with white people.

In the Indian Treaty of Washington of 1835, provisions were made to remove Michigan Indians to reservations west of the Mississippi River. But unlike the Cherokees, Choctaws, and other eastern tribes, few Ottawas and Chippewas made the move, and those who did, including those who had fled to Canada, returned to Michigan after a short time. Michigan Territorial Governor Lewis Cass's policy toward the Indians was positively benign. So also was his Indian Agent's, Henry Schoolcraft, who married an Indian princess.

TRAVERSE CITY'S FIRST HOSPITAL

The first well-equipped hospital in the Traverse City area was opened in the spring of 1901 by a doctor named Victor Hugo Sturm. It stood on the hill behind what is now Tom's Shopping Center on the corner of M-22 and M-72 in Greilickville. It was known as Grand Traverse Hospital, or "Shelternook", as it was sometimes called.

Dr. Sturm was born in Germany in 1838. His father, also a physician, was a surgeon on the staff of Napolean Bonaparte. His son was named for the great French novelist Victor Hugo, who, according to family tradition, was his godfather and held him in his arms when he was baptized. His mother died in Berlin, and his father came with his son to Cincinnati, where he practiced medicine for many years.

After graduation from medical college, Dr. Victor Sturm also established a medical practice in that city, specializing in homeopathy. Later, in his 40s, he gave up his practice, took a job with a pharmaceutical company in St. Louis, Mo., and traveled the country by train for 25 years as their representative. In the late 1890s he moved to Traverse City and married his second wife, Sylvia Robbins of Reed City. They had a daughter who lived only a few days and was buried at Oakland Cemetery.

Shortly after coming to Traverse City, Dr. Sturm incorporated the Grand Traverse Hospital Association, of which he was elected President, and bought the already existing Grand Traverse Hospital from Dr. Hurley. It was a three-story, multi-gabled wooden building inadequate in facilities and equipment to the needs of the growing Traverse City community, and Dr. Sturm spent a lot of money bringing it up to current standards.

A few years later, the *Traverse City Evening Record* ran the following story:

> *Dr. Sturm of the Grand Traverse hospital has completed the armamentarium of the hospital to perfection. He had added an entirely new operating table of the latest design and complete hot air treatment apparatus, including the body and joint ovens and many other appliances—in fact, everything necessary to a strictly first class hospital. The hospital is open to the medical profession at large. Graduated and experienced nurses are in charge of the sick.*

The year of 1909 was a busy one for the hospital, the *Evening Record* reported. The total number of cases admitted was 144, including 85 operations, 59 medical cases, 2047 treatment days, and only 10 deaths.

Dr. Sturm was able to spend only limited time at the hospital— he was still traveling for the St. Louis pharmaceutical company. On Dec. 28, 1909, he died at the age of 71, on a train near Mason City, Iowa. After that, the hospital was operated on a lease basis by different people until 1915, when the building was destroyed by fire. At that time, only three patients were there. All were removed safely.

The loss left Traverse City without any hospital facilities— until that same year Dr. James Decker Munson, Superintendent of Traverse City State Hospital (known as the Asylum), came to the rescue and renovated an apartment building on the State Hospital grounds at the corner of 11th Street and South Elmwood Avenue and turned it over to local doctors for treating their patients.

A new general hospital, named after James Decker Munson, opened in 1926.

THE OLDEST HOUSE IN TOWN

The distinction of being the oldest house in Traverse City belongs to a modest one-story bungalow at 413 Washington Street. It was built in 1858 by early settler, Morgan Bates, who came here that same year and established the settlement's first newspaper, *Grand Traverse Herald*. At that time the 400 block of Washington Street was still in the woods at some distance from the tiny village, and for several years Morgan's was the only house in that area. In his "Glimpse of the Village in 1862", Morgan's nephew, Thomas Bates wrote, "A small school stood on the present site of the Park Place Annex, and in the far-off suburbs to the southeast Morgan Bates had ventured to defy the wilderness and build a house…"

Morgan Bates sold the house to Thomas, who moved in with his bride, Martha E. Cram, on their wedding day, on May 5, 1867. Thomas built the first sidewalk in town, a boardwalk from his house to the Park Place Hotel.

Over the years, the Bates house grew by additions. Originally a three-room structure, it now has ten rooms with no less that eight outside doors. Before the present cedar shakes, the exterior was white clapboard with green shutters. The shutters came from Rev. Peter Dougherty's New Mission Church at Omena.

FAME AND THE FAMOUS

SILENT CAL COOLIDGE AND THE BIG CHERRY PIE

C alvin Coolidge, 30th President of the United States, was a man of few words, some of them well chosen. The following is a good illustration of his taciturnity and wit:

At one of the big White House dinners Coolidge found himself seated beside a diplomat's attractive wife. The lady opened the conversation, saying, "Mr. President, I have made a bet with a friend of mine. She bet me that I wouldn't get three words out of you."

"You lose," said the President, with a smile.

In 1926, the Grand Traverse region's cherry crop was so bountiful and of such excellent quality that the growers wanted to let everyone know about it—including the President. One of them was Frank Burkhart, local orchardist and packer, who suggested: "Let's bake a big cherry pie and send it to President Coolidge." And the idea caught on.

The huge pie, three feet in diameter, was put together and baked at the Hawkins Bakery in Traverse City, using a special pie tin with interior sections so the contents wouldn't slide around. It took around five thousand Montmorency cherries—42 pounds—to fill the deep-dish pie. After baking, it was left to cool in the bakery's street window for everyone to see.

The big question now arose: How best to get it to the President, who was vacationing at a private summer estate in the Adirondack Mountains of New York. That problem was solved when Wallace Keep, a classmate of Coolidge at Amherst College, volunteered to accompany the pie and present it to the President; and Frank Burkhart offered his new Lincoln automobile to carry it, with his son Hugh as chauffeur.

They set out with the pie on Saturday, August 14. Their route took them to Detroit, then across Canada to Niagara Falls. On Sunday Hugh was stopped for speeding at 47 m.p.h., but the motorcycle cop waved them on when they told him about their mission. They arrived at the mountain resort on Tuesday, August 17, and were met at the gate by the Secret Service and the President's personal secretary, Edward T. Clark.

At a formal meeting next day, Keep and Burkhart presented the pie to the President "on behalf of the citizens of the Grand Traverse region of Michigan." It was said that Coolidge "appeared unusually pleased and almost jocose with his guests."

In a note dated September 3, 1926, to Wallace Keep, President Coolidge wrote: "My dear Keep: I am very glad to make written as well as verbal acknowledgement of the kindness of the people of Traverse City in sending to me the cherry pie which you brought in person. In spite of the long journey it was still delicious, and this can probably be attributed to the exceptionally fine quality of the cherries of which it was made."

This was the first of a long tradition of sending cherry pie to the President of the United States.

RED GRANGE SPOKE HERE

They called him the Galloping Ghost because when you tried to tackle him, he simply wasn't there. Many of his would-be tacklers never managed to lay a hand on him. In his day, he was the best broken-field runner in football and probably the best remembered halfback in the history of the game—the prototype of Gale Sayers and Barry Sanders.

Harold Edward "Red" Grange was born in Forksville, Pennsylvania, in 1903. He grew up there and in Wheaton, Illinois, where he starred in high school track and football. In 1922 he enrolled at the University of Illinois, and was named All-American by Walter Camp in all three of his varsity seasons. In 1924 he became a national idol, leading Illinois to a Big Ten championship win over Michigan, 39-14. In that contest he opened the game with a 100-yard kickoff return, scored three more times in the next ten minutes, added a fifth touchdown in the second half, and passed for another.

His professional career with the Chicago Bears was somewhat disappointing. He was plagued by injuries and sat out the entire 1928 season and parts of others, but his fame still drew record crowds. He retired as a player in 1935.

Red was still with the Bears as backfield coach in 1936, when he was invited to speak at Traverse City to a crowd of high school football players and their coaches on Wednesday, October 21. The meeting was sponsored by the Sinclair Oil Company and organized by their local manager Ned Kehoe. Letters were sent to the coaches of high school teams in northern Michigan from Reed City to the Straits, urging them to bring their entire squads.

On Wednesday morning Kehoe drove to Grand Rapids to meet the great athlete at the railroad station and bring him to Traverse City. After lunch at the Park Place Hotel he was taken on a tour of the city and to meet Coach Lee Orr and the Trojans at Thirlby Field.

"If you can block, your team is going to score," he told the boys. "If you can tackle, the other team isn't going to score." Grange always gave a lot of credit to his blockers. They made it easy for him, he said.

Grange was guest of honor at a dinner for high school officials and others at the Park Place. Then at 7:15 the high school marching band and a large delegation of students called at the hotel to escort him to the high school auditorium. The place was packed. Every one of the 17 coaches was present and all but two brought their teams. The Master of Ceremonies was Lew Holliday, head of the *Record-Eagle's* sports department. In response to his questions Grange entertained the audience with anecdotes of his football years at Illinois, where he was both captain and quarterback of the team.

His greatest thrill, he said, was not the great Michigan game, but a game against the University of Pennsylvania in 1925. The Illinois team was relatively weak that year, having lost four games in a row. But Penn underestimated the Galloping Ghost, who ran wild all afternoon before a crowd of 70,000, gaining 363 yards and three touchdowns in a 24-2 victory over the powerhouse of the East. He said that nothing he experienced before or since compared with the satisfaction of that day.

In his final message to the several hundred high school athletes, Grange said:

"The boy who smokes, stays out late at night, and otherwise neglects to care for himself may be able to stay on the team, but he is only two thirds as good as he would be if he observed sensible training rules which, after all, means simple and sane living."

BUFFALO BILL WAS HERE

It was a banner day in Traverse City history. With the possible exception of Christmas and the Fourth of July it was by far the most exciting day of the year.

On Tuesday, July 19, 1898, Buffalo Bill Cody brought his famous Wild West show to the city for an afternoon and evening performance. It arrived on the early Chicago & Northeastern train and paraded through the streets en route to the Fairgrounds between Thirteenth and Fourteenth streets (where Thirlby Field stands today). It was led by the great man himself in his traditional fringed buckskin jacket, cowboy hat and silver spurs, white handlebar mustache, goatee and all—smiling and waving at the cheering crowd.

Later a reporter for the *Morning Record* pulled out all stops in describing the famous scout of the western plains: "Father Time has sprinkled his flowing locks with silver threads, but he still has a distinguished bearing, perfect physical manhood, and a face of great character and expression which is an interesting study. He rides his horse like a Centaur and a grace that lends a charm that is intensified by the associations connected with his brilliant career." Wow!

Intermittent rain showers reduced the size of the crowd for the evening performance but nonetheless failed to dampen its enthusiasm.

Buffalo Bill's real name was William Frederick Cody. He was born in 1846 near Davenport, Iowa, but spent most of his early years in the American "Wild West", hunting and trapping and supplying buffalo meat for the railroad construction crews. During the Civil War he served as an army scout on the western plains.

In 1872, the "dime novelist" Ned Buntline persuaded Cody to appear on the stage, and in 1882 he organized his Wild West Show, touring all over America and Europe for many years. It had many imitators.

Buffalo Bill died in Denver in 1917 and was buried on Lookout Mountain near Golden, Colorado.

HOME RUN BUNDY BRIEF

Bundy Brief was Traverse City's homegrown baseball hero. He was the only local boy to make it all the way to the big leagues.

Bundy was a natural. He started out playing baseball here on the sandlots when he was four or five. He could play any position, including pitcher, though he preferred the outfield or first base. The first mention of him in the *Record-Eagle* was in 1905, when his team, the Traverse City Hustlers, played Oval Wood Dish and lost 10-2, in spite of Bundy's spectacular hitting and fielding.

In 1910 he was playing stellar ball for Traverse City in the Michigan State league. A big shy loose-jointed kid standing over six feet tall and weighing 185 pounds, Bundy's first big break was in 1912 when the St. Louis Browns signed him up after one of their scouts watched him play—he was hitting home runs all over the park.

So Bundy caught the train here for St. Louis with all the family waving him goodbye at the station. He got as far as Grand Rapids, then caught the next train back to Traverse City. He was homesick.

To ease the pain of parting with his family, his brother Tom accompanied him to St. Louis and stayed in a hotel for the first season. He played two seasons with the Browns, 1912 and 1913, hitting .310 and .273.

In 1915 he went to Chicago and alternated with Jack Fournier at first base. Three other White Sox teammates were Hap Felsch, Shoeless Joe Jackson, and Eddie Cicotte. They later became notorious when they helped throw the 1919 World Series to Cincinnati in the Chicago "Black Sox" scandal. The great Eddie Collins and Buck Weaver weren't in on the take; neither was Bundy Brief. A frequent double play during the 1915 season was Collins to Weaver to Brief.

Bundy finished his big league career at Pittsburg in 1917, batting only .217.

But for the next ten years Bundy burned up the best of the minor leagues, setting a home run record for the Pacific Coast League. His best years were with the Kansas City Blues; in 1922 he hit 42 homers, a record for the American Association; in 1921 he drove in 191 runs, a record that still stands. He closed out his playing career with the Milwaukee Brewers, then an American Association team, and retired in 1928.

During the early 1930s Bundy operated a gas station in Traverse City; its logo was two crossed bats. He also wrote a sports column for the *Record-Eagle*.

Northern Creamery named an ice cream treat for him: a scoop of vanilla dipped in chocolate on a wooden stick. They were called "Home Run Bundies."

Bundy and his wife and daughter moved to Milwaukee in 1933, where he took a position as city recreation director, a job he held until his retirement in 1963.

Bundy was born in Big Rapids in 1892, and came to Traverse City at the age of three. His real name was Anthony Vincent Grezckowski. The origin of his nickname "Bundy" is still a mystery. But the story of how he got his surname "Brief" is a delight.

Shortly after the turn of the century, the story goes, his oldest brother Tom applied for work at one of the local factories, probably Oval Wood Dish. The foreman asked his name, and Tom told him.

"Aw, that's too long," the foreman said, and turning to the timekeeper, said, "Make it brief."

So the timekeeper wrote down "Tom Brief." That was all right with Tom, who was getting tired anyway of having people say "How's that again?" when asked to give his name. It was all right, too, with the whole family—father, mother, brothers and sisters—who decided to make it easy for everybody and changed their name to Brief.

Bundy died in Milwaukee on February, 1963, and his wife Rhea brought him back to his beloved hometown and buried him in Oakwood Cemetery. She lies there now beside him, and their daughter Barbara Seahill lies nearby.

TRACKING JOHN DILLINGER

I̲s it true that the notorious bank robber John Dillinger was in Traverse City some time before or after his daring escape from the Crown Point, Indiana, jail on March 3, 1934?

On March 5, 1934, the following story appeared in the *Traverse City Record Eagle:*

BULLETIN

Suspicion that John Dillinger, escaped Indiana prisoner, may have passed through Traverse City this afternoon, was aroused when Ben H. Koenig and G. W. Powers noticed a Ford Sedan or coach, wine-colored, containing a white man and a Negro, drive north on Union Street and turn east on Front shortly after noon today.

Local officers were immediately notified and started in pursuit of the car. State police left immediately for the north and other local officers also gave chase. Elk Rapids and Charlevoix were both asked to be on the lookout for the car.

The car carried the Michigan license X-10235 to a Peerless car in Detroit.

Both Koenig, a local builder, and Powers, an insurance agency owner, were solidly credible citizens, and it's true that Dillinger's companion in the jail break was a black man named Youngblood. But, as everyone knows, eye-witness accounts are often faulty. In any case, since there was no follow-up story in the paper, we must assume that the cops never caught up with the wine-colored car and its occupants, whoever they were.

However, on page 286 of a book entitled *American Agent*, published in 1936, FBI Agent Melvin Purvis, Dillinger's nemesis, wrote this: "Mrs. Anna Campbell Steve, sister of John Hamilton, was sentenced to serve four months at the Grand Traverse, Mich. Jail for harboring Dillinger and Hamilton."

The Great Depression of the 1930s was open season on banks for such hoodlums as Dillinger, Alvin Karpis, Pretty Boy Floyd, and Bonnie and Clyde. They robbed banks because, as Willie Horton explained, that's where the money was; nobody else had any. Some of them became folk heroes in the tradition of Robin Hood and Jesse James, who "robbed the rich to help the poor."

Dillinger's sensational escape from the jail at Crown Point, Indiana, on March 3, 1934, aroused a hue and cry as widespread as any in history. The whole nation was engaged in a furor of speculation about where he might turn up next. He was reported seen simultaneously in eight or ten widely separated places all over the country. If the reports were true, he would have had to be as ubiquitous as Santa Claus, Kilroy, or a ghost. The FBI listed him as Public Enemy No. 1.

Dillinger was finally run to earth a few months later and died in an ambush by a fusillade from G-men and other cops in front of the Biograph Theater in Chicago as he reached for his .380 automatic pistol in his right-hand pants pocket. He had been betrayed for $5,000 by Anna Steve, who later became famous as the "Woman in Red." Steve, the landlady of Dillinger's girl, Polly Hamilton, had tipped off the FBI as to Dillinger's whereabouts. The cops found out later that, while they were chasing him all over the country, he'd spent most of the time in Chicago. Incidentally, Dillinger was said to have escaped from the Crown Point jail using a wooden gun, but FBI reports show that a real gun was smuggled to him by a confederate.

But what about the mystery woman, Anna Campbell Steve? Was she sentenced to serve four months in the Grand Traverse County jail for harboring Dillinger and Hamilton, as Purvis alleges in his book? If that's true, then, by all the rules of logic, the two must have spent some time in this vicinity.

But if that is true, why is there no mention of it in the *Traverse City Record Eagle*? Such a sensational story in our little town would be a cinch to make the front page. Yet a diligent search of the newspaper files and the circuit court records has failed to turn up a single word about Steve and her alleged felony. Did Purvis get his wires crossed? Did such a woman every exist? You be the judge.

JACK DEMPSEY KEPT HIS PROMISE

In 1919, Jack Dempsey, the "Manasa Mauler," won the world's heavyweight boxing title at Toledo, Ohio, from Jess Willard, the Kansas giant. In this bout, Dempsey' most famous, he knocked Willard down seven times in the first round before delivering the *coup de grace* in the third. Several weeks before the fight Dempsey promised Otto Floto, one of the owners of the Sells-Floto circus that if he defeated Willard he would make several appearances at the circus. When Floto approached him after the fight, Dempsey said he would keep his word, and that he would open the show at Newark, New Jersey. Before the opening date, however, Dempsey's mother was taken seriously ill in Salt Lake City, and the champion asked that his appearance be postponed so he could spend time with her. The request was readily granted.

In the meantime, Dempsey and his manager, Jack Kearns, were being deluged with offers for his services at figures beyond expectations. A Chicago syndicate offered the champion $15,000 a week to head a big vaudeville company for a fall and winter season, with the stipulation that he be permitted to appear with the circus first, and thus keep his promise.

Dempsey's arrangement with the circus was that he appear in several Michigan cities, including Traverse City. And he was here, on Tuesday, August 12, 1919, riding on one of the splendid four hundred horses along with dozens of animals in cages—including a hippopotamus in his water tank—and lots of clowns and pretty girls in tights, as the long parade marched majestically to the music of the big brass band to the fairgrounds. Dempsey was the main attraction. He and his sparring partner staged a replica of the Dempsey-Willard fight, making it as realistic as possible in a genuine elevated boxing ring with padded ropes, opening and closing bell, and referee.

AD WOLGAST

Ad Wolgast was the world's lightweight boxing champion from 1910 to 1912. In 1910 he won the title from Bat Nelson, the Durable Dane, in a match that was scheduled for 45 rounds. But Nelson was in such bad shape at the end of 40 that the referee stopped the fight. In 1912 Wolgast lost the title to Willie Ritchie on a technicality.

In another fight, Wolgast against Mexican Joe Rivers, both men were knocked cold simultaneously by right-hand punches, and the referee started counting. But when it became obvious that neither man could rise in time, he tucked Wolgast under one arm and supported him while he counted Rivers out, justifying his action on the grounds that Wolgast had landed his punch first.

So what's all that got to do with the history of the Grand Traverse region? Well, Wolgast was born and raised in Cadillac, which of course is part of the region.

In the summer of 1911, on a pleasure outing with three friends in his automobile, Wolgast narrowly missed a horse and buggy on State Street near the Park Place Hotel. The horse reared and threw its driver, a local young lady, out of the buggy. Ad and his friends picked her up, dusted her off, and acted like perfect gentlemen—so the *Record-Eagle* reported—and the lady wasn't hurt.

Next day, however, the newspaper printed a letter from an irate citizen, criticizing the paper for praising the conduct of a "despicable prizefighter" and suggested that Wolgast and his companions should have been run out of town. The writer was obviously no boxing fan.

Ernest Hemingway used Ad Wolgast as a model for the broken-down punch-drunk prizefighter Ad Francis in one of his best short stories, "The Battler."

Another great fighter from Cadillac was Stanley Ketchel, who won the middleweight championship in 1908. Ketchel was the perfect middleweight, but he had the brass to challenge heavyweight champion Jack Johnson, arguably the best fighter of all time, who outweighed him by 35 pounds.

The understanding was that Johnson would "carry" Ketchel for a number of rounds to give the fans their money's worth. But Ketchel pulled a fast one and knocked the champion down in the 12th round. That made Johnson mad. He got up and knocked Ketchel out with one terrific blow.

WALTER HAGEN LIVED HERE

Walter C. Hagen, one of golf's greatest players, spent most of his retirement years at his home near Traverse City. In 1954 he bought 30 acres at the south end of Long Lake and lived there until his death in 1969. A familiar figure in the Traverse City area, he lent his support to the Walter Hagen Invitational golf tournament held annually at the Traverse City Golf and Country Club, and later, at Elmbrook Golf Course.

"The Haig", as he was often called, was not only a great golfer, he was also one of the game's most colorful players. He was a *bon vivant*, a lover of fine food and drink and high-spirited living.

"I never wanted to be a millionaire," he said. "I just wanted to live like one." He took pride in saying that he was the first professional golfer to make a million dollars, and spend two.

Two of the greatest achievements were lowering the social barriers that excluded professional golfers from the clubhouse, and making the game popular as a spectator sport worldwide from St. Andrews to Singapore.

"The golf pros owe more to him than they do to the sand wedge," noted one sports columnist. "He took them out of overalls and put them in the company of counselors and kings."

One of the best stories about him—among a multitude of them—was about the time he played an exhibition in Nassau with the Duke of Windsor, the former King Edward VIII, in the gallery. At one point in the round, Sir Walter surveyed a chip shot from off the green, turned to His Highness and said, "Eddie, hold the pin for me," and Eddie, with a smile, willingly complied. His common touch and joy of life made him one of the best-loved players of the game. He played it with a flair that has never been matched.

He also was a master of psychology and showmanship, and he used these tools—along with his great ability as a scrambler—to unnerve and defeat many a foe, even on days when his won game wasn't particularly sharp.

He was a very good swinger, a great putter, and a man who had the almost uncanny ability to hit "impossible" recovery shots to the green (like Tiger Woods) and then sink a birdie to beat the opponent who was never out of the fairway.

The Haig won two U.S. Opens, four British Opens, and five PGA Opens—the last four in succession—plus dozens of lesser titles. His largest single paycheck came in 1926, when he earned $7,600 for beating the immortal Bobby Jones in an exhibition match, the only time these two golfing greats came together.

Another golf great, Gene Sarazen, once wrote: "All the professionals who have a chance to go after the big money today should give thanks to Walter Hagen. It was Walter who made professional golf what it is."

CUSTER WAS HERE

It is said that more books and articles have been written about George Armstrong Custer than any other American except Abraham Lincoln. The two words that best describe Custer are flamboyant and fearless. Both led to his untimely end.

Shortly after the two-day bloody cavalry battle of Trevillian Station, where Custer's Michigan Brigade suffered severe casualties, Custer requested a 20-day furlough because of illness, and it was granted. He left for Washington on July 13, 1864, picked up his wife Libbie and took the train for Monroe, Michigan. Finding Libbie's father and mother already gone to Traverse City, they followed them by lake steamer the next day.

Monroe was the birthplace of Elizabeth (Libbie) Bacon; and there in Monroe, Custer, after a long and tempestuous courtship, married her on February 9, 1864. Her father, Daniel S. Bacon, was one of Monroe's distinguished citizens, a circuit court judge and Michigan state senator. He had been dubious at first about Custer's ability to support a wife on an army lieutenant's pay, but when Custer was promoted in 1863 to brigadier general, Judge Bacon gave consent to the marriage. Over the years the Bacon family had spent considerable time in Traverse City, where Judge Bacon had family ties and business interests: his nephew Albert Bacon lived there.

On July 19, 1864, and at 4:20 in the morning the Custers took the Michigan Southern & Northern Railroad to Detroit, where they boarded the *Iron City,* a paddlewheel excursion steamer, transferring in Port Huron to the much faster propeller *Oneida*, arriving at Northport on the evening of July 22, and stayed there overnight at the Traverse Bay Hotel.

After visiting relatives and friends in Traverse City, they returned to Monroe and were back in the U.S. Capitol on July 29. Custer reported for duty the next day.

MURDER, MAYHEM, AND TRICKERY

MASS MURDER AT BLISSWOOD

One of Michigan's most horrifying and perplexing mass murders took place in late June, 1968, at the private summer resort of Blisswood in northwest Michigan, two miles north of Good Hart. An entire family of six—Richard C. Robison, 42, and his wife Shirley, 40; sons Richard, 19, Gary, 17, Randy, 12, and daughter Susie, 8—was annihilated, gunned down at their summer cottage on Lake Michigan.

One of the bodies was discovered on Monday, July 22, by caretaker Chauncey A. Bliss. He had been alerted by close neighbors of the Robisons who complained of a foul odor in the vicinity of the Robison cottage. They thought it might be coming from a dead animal inside.

The caretaker wasn't surprised that the door was locked and the windows curtained. The last time he had seen the family was on June 23 when Robison had told him they were about to leave on a trip. With his caretaker's key he unlocked and opened the door. What he saw inside made his blood run cold. Quickly he closed the door, relocked it and hastened to call the police.

Within a short time, half a dozen police officers arrived at the scene. They entered the cottage through what one of the officers described as a "wall of flies". They found dead bodies all over the place.

Shirley Robison's body lay on the living room floor covered with a blanket. Three of the children lay in a group in the hallway to the bedrooms. Dick Robison lay dead in one of the bedrooms together with one of the children. All had been shot in the head. The police also found a bloodstained hammer on the living room floor, and one set of bloody footprints.

An autopsy conducted at Petoskey the next day revealed that all had been shot by bullets of two different calibers, identified later as from a .25 Beretta handgun and AR-7 .22 long rifle. Susie, the eight-year-old, had also been bludgeoned with a hammer.

After months of intense investigations, the authorities pieced together a plausible scenario. They were convinced that this was a premeditated, cold-blooded mass murder by a lone gunman who wanted Robison dead and planned to leave no witness alive. The evidence suggested that on that fateful evening the family was gathered around a table in the living room, playing a game of cards. The first shots came from a .22 caliber rifle through a window near the door. The killer then entered the cottage and finished his grisly work with the handgun.

On the day after the autopsy Shirley Robison's brother, Joe Scolero who was Robison's business associate chartered a flight from Detroit to Petoskey to talk with the police. Scolero told them he was shocked by the murders. "We were more like brothers than business partners," he said.

The police listed him as a possible suspect, but in a routine check they turned up some troubling evidence. He had a heated telephone argument with Robison on the morning of the murders. He couldn't account for eleven hours of that day. He owned the same kind of guns used in the murders.

Almost from the beginning, the police had put together a profile of the killer. They believed that he was possibly a friend of the family, that he was familiar with the cottage and premises, perhaps had stayed there as a friend. Scolero fit the profile.

The murder weapons were never found. But the investigation dragged on and Scolero was never charge. Five years later Scolero committed suicide with a handgun, but not with a Beretta. He left a note that he was innocent of the Robison murders.

A TRAVERSE CITY TRAGEDY

It happened in the early 1860s, when Traverse City was still a small town and nearly everybody worked at the Hannah, Lay & Company sawmill on the bay or in the company store.

One of the mill workers was Thomas Green, who lived with his wife and five children on Bay Street in what was then called Slabtown. Green was a dependable worker, but he had a bad accident at the mill one day and one of his legs was crushed. Since Traverse City had no medical facilities in those days, and only one doctor,

Perry Hannah decided to move the injured man to Chicago for medical attention. He was taken there aboard the company's ship *Allegheny* and lodged in St. Luke's Hospital.

Perry Hannah's partner, Albert Tracy Lay, lived in Chicago and managed the company's business there. He made frequent trips to the hospital to visit the patient and to see that everything possible was being done for him.

One day he found Green almost despondent, very low in strength and spirits. He had had a terrible dream that night, Green told him. In the dream he saw his two sons lying dead and thought they had been drowned.

Lay did his best to reassure the sick man, saying that dreams had no substance and that he was sure nothing had happened to his boys. Lay promised to bring Green the latest news from Traverse City as soon as the *Allegheny* docked; she was due to arrive at Chicago that very day.

Soon after leaving the hospital Lay saw the boat in the distance and hurried down to the wharf to await its arrival. As he approached the dock he saw Perry Hannah standing on the deck with a deeply troubled face.

What was the news from Traverse City? Lay asked him.

Terrible news, Hannah told him. Tom Green's two boys had drowned a few days before.

"Oh, no!" cried Lay. "It can't be!"

But Hannah assured him it was true.

Hannah said that the two boys, after attending school, went down to the bay shore, just below the mouth of the river, to go swimming. With them was Sedgewick Stevens, the son of General I. T. Stevens, who was visiting the General's brother, Oscar Stevens, Registrar at the Traverse City Land Office.

None of the boys was ever again seen alive. They had been victims of the treacherous "deep hole" offshore, as others had been before them. The bodies were recovered, and the two Green boys were buried in a single coffin at the old cemetery on Sixth Street; Sedgewick's body was returned to Washington for burial.

With a heavy heart Tracy Lay returned to the hospital, sorely troubled about how to break the terrible news to the anxious father.

Fate, however, spared him that ordeal. Another messenger had preceded him, leading Thomas Green by the hand to join his boys "on the other side."

KALEVA BANK ROBBERY

About eleven o'clock in the morning of January 5, 1933, four armed men drove into the village of Kaleva on the pine plains near Manistee. They parked their 1930 Buick sedan in front of the post office across the street from the Kaleva State Bank. One of them jumped out of the car carrying a shotgun and entered the post office. Brandishing the gun, he ordered the postmaster and three civilians to put up their hands and keep quiet. "Nothing bad is going to happen if you do exactly as I say," he told them.

Meanwhile, the other three bandits got out of the car, crossed the street and entered the building.

Only two men were inside: Wallace Haines, a local farmer, and the bank's cashier, Ellsworth Billman. Haines was in the process of settling an account with Billman. The cashier had just turned his back to the front door to look at an interest table on a nearby desk when the three men entered. One stood guard at the door, and the other two approached the teller's cage. One covered Haines with a pistol. The other said to Billman, "You know what we're here for."

Billman looked up from the chart and leaned forward.

The gunman cursed him, snarling, "Don't touch that alarm!" and shot Billman through the heart, killing him instantly. The two robbers then entered the open vault and scooped up $3,000 in cash and about $7,000 in negotiable bonds, which they stuffed into a cloth sack. All three then ran out the door and across the street to the car, where the man with the shotgun was backing slowly out of the post office door. Then all four piled into the car and sped out of town. Minutes later, a carload of Kaleva businessmen armed to the teeth roared out of town in hot pursuit. They failed to catch up with the bandits, and the last word received from the chase came from a few miles south of Kaleva, where several farmers, alerted by State

Police radio bulletins, reported that the bandit car had crossed M-55 heading south, with the posse less than five minutes behind.

Thus began one of the greatest manhunts in Michigan history.

All through the night and the best part of next day, the cops and the robbers were engaged in a game of hide and seek, with alarms and excursions, unfounded rumors, missed opportunities, and close encounters when the hunted barely slipped through the hands of the hunters.

One such incident involved State Police Captain Earl Hathaway of Traverse City, who was in tactical command of the pursuit. He spotted the bandits' car that night and gave chase, only to find it abandoned by the robbers, who fled into a dense woods at the side of the road. A search of the trunk revealed a pistol, sawed-off shotgun, rifle, bullet-proof vest, and the stolen bonds, but not the cash. With the fugitives on foot in the bush, all police cars were concentrated around Baldwin and the Lake-Newaygo county lines. Now it was only a matter of time.

On Saturday afternoon, after listening to police reports on his radio, a farmer named Ben McGahan loaded his deer rifle and stood watch at his house. Half an hour later he spotted four men in the distance, walking in single file, approaching his house. He watched them until they disappeared into a small cedar swamp. Then, knowing where they would probably emerge, he took a position outside and waited.

When they broke cover, he shouldered the rifle and ordered them to drop their weapons. Instead, they turned and ran. McGahan fired two shots, both of which struck the man bringing up the rear. Then he ran back to the house and telephoned the State Police.

The cops arrived within minutes. They found the wounded man groaning in the brush, and within an hour caught up with the other three fugitives, who surrendered without a fight. They were a sorry lot, wet, cold and hungry—like kids with all the starch gone out of them. All were in their twenties, all from Indiana, where they had acquired long criminal records and done prison time.

All were tried for murder and were sentenced to prison for life.

TRAVERSE CITY'S FIRST MURDER CASE

On June 6, 1861, the following story appeared in Traverse City's first newspaper, the *Grand Traverse Herald*. It was written by its editor and publisher, Morgan Bates.

SUPPOSE MURDER—our usually quiet and moral town was thrown into a state of great excitement on Monday morning last by the report that Nicholas Frankinburger, a German in the employ of Hannah, Lay & Co. had been murdered by his wife, through the instrumentality of poison, aided and abetted by her paramour, Paul Riter, also a German, and in the employ of Hannah, Lay & Co.

They were both arrested and and committed to await the result of an inquest, which was held by Justice of the Peace, Morgan Bates. The jury returned a verdict that, in their opinion, the deceased came to his death from the effects of poison taken with his food on Sunday afternoon, June 2, 1861, by the wife of the deceased, Mary Frankinburger, that an unlawful intimacy has been known to exist between Paul Riter and the wife of the deceased, and that such intimacy may have prompted the act, by collusion or otherwise."

Bates added the Drs. Scheterly and Goodale had performed a post mortem on the deceased and that the stomach and its contents had been taken to Ann Arbor by Dr. Goodale to be analyzed.

On July 7, 1861, Bates reported as follows:

The examination of Mary Frankinburger and Paul Riter, for the murder of Nicholas Frankinburger was held before Justice Bates on Thursday and Friday last and resulted in the commitment of the parties for trial at the August term of the Circuit Court for Grand Traverse County. The contents of the stomach were analyzed by Professor Douglas of The University of Michigan and large quantities of arsenic found.

This was doubtless mixed with the food which constituted his dinner on Sunday, the first of June. He died on Sunday night. Paul Riter, the paramour of Mrs. Frankinburger, made a special trip to Chicago and returned on the Saturday evening previous to the murder, and had a brief interview with Mrs. Frankinburger. The supposition is that he procured the poison in Chicago and gave it to Mrs. Frankinburger at that time.

The trial of the two defendants in Circuit Court in August was held by a long-time friend of Bates, Judge Flavius Josephus Littlejohn. Nevertheless, Bates wrote a blistering criticism of the proceedings and the verdict. In his own words:

Mary Frankinburger was tried for poisoning her husband, Nicholas Frankinburger. The judge ruled out all the circumstantial evidence, and in the absence of positive testimony to convict, the Jury acquitted her, though there is no doubt of her guilt. Such a ruling on the part of the Judge may be in accordance with the technicalities of the law but contrary to justice and common sense; and under it courts are a humbug, lawyers useless members of society and judges of no earthly account.

In the case of Paul Riter, a nol pros *was entered and the prisoner discharged as all the evidence against him was circumstantial, though of so strong a character as to convince everyone of his guilt who was at all familiar with the case.*

Morgan Bates, a friend of Horace Greeley, was well known in the national publishing and political arena. He held various political offices in Grand Traverse County and served as Lieutenant Governor of Michigan from 1868 to 1874. He was known as a man of strong convictions and plain speech, mincing no words.

THE BOUNCING CROQUET BALL

Mrs. Vaughn didn't really believe in ghosts. But she had a nervous disposition, so it didn't help matters when, shortly after she and her family moved into the house at 406 Elmwood Street, she began to hear strange noises late at night. The queer thing was that the disturbances occurred only on Friday nights, when she was alone in the house with her three small boys. (For that matter, Mrs. Vaughn was alone every night except on Sundays. Her husband Fred worked at the mill at Cedar and could get home only on weekends.)

It had seemed a very nice house when they first moved in, on a Sunday in late July, 1902. They had rented the house from Mrs. David J. Dokey, a very lovely woman, Mrs. Vaughn thought. But it was on a Friday night of that same week that she first heard the noises. They woke her up around midnight.

It was a hollow, booming sort of sound, as though someone was beating slowly and rhythmically on an empty wooden barrel. Mrs. Vaughn lay in bed in the dark for awhile, listening to it. It seemed to be coming from somewhere upstairs (she and the boys slept in the two downstairs bedrooms) but she couldn't be sure. It made the whole house tremble.

After a while, mastering her fear, she got up and lit a lamp. Without disturbing the children, who were fast asleep, she made a thorough search of the house, room by room. She found nothing. Curiously, the sounds ceased as soon as she reached the upstairs landing, and they were heard no more that night.

Later, Mrs. Vaughn told a neighbor that the ghost must be a very timid one that didn't want to be seen. They both laughed, nervously.

On Sunday Mrs. Vaughn and her husband made another thorough inspection of the house, inside and out, nailing down loose boards, securing shutters, and rearranging everything that might be causing the noises. But it wasn't any good. On Friday night she was awakened again by the boom-boom-boom, and it happened every

Friday night for the next three months. It seemed to Mrs. Vaughn that she might be getting used to it—the pattern was always the same.

But then, on the following Friday night she got the scare of her life. She awoke to a different kind of sound: a series of raps or sharp knocks. It sounded as if a croquet ball had started to roll downstairs, hitting every step along the way.

That did it. Mrs. Vaughn got the kids up and dressed and together they took refuge at the house of a neighbor, Mrs. Will Neason. Next morning she told a *Record-Eagle* reported that she would not spend another night in that house.

The reporter also learned, while talking to the neighbors, that the house had an unsavory reputation. Three families had lived there for short periods of time, then moved out for no apparent reason. After the Vaughns left, the house remained vacant for several months, but eventually Mrs. Dokey was able to rent it again. And insofar as is known, the ghost was never seen or heard from again.

Since it was a very timid ghost, maybe it just got cold feet and went away.

EXPLOSION IN GRAND TRAVERSE BAY

A strange thing happened in Grand Traverse Bay one day in June of 1899. On a spot opposite the Grand Rapids & Indiana Railroad depot (at the foot of Park Street), the water seemed to be boiling. This lasted for several minutes. Then, a gigantic burp broke the surface, lifting a large volume of water four feet high. Several people witnessed the phenomenon. They were astonished. They didn't know what to make of it.

The same thing happened a couple of weeks later. But this time, after bubbling furiously for several minutes, the water was lifted by the final eruption in a column twenty feet high. It scared the daylights out of a boatload of fishermen anchored nearby; they rowed ashore in record time.

On June 13, 1899, the story made the front page of the *Morning Record* under the headline "THE BAY DISTURBED."

The annual explosion in the bay opposite the GR&I depot occurred yesterday . . . . These submarine disturbances have been a mystery for many years and as yet no explanation has been made to account for the disturbances. The gushing of the water was observed by several persons yesterday.

Another brief story in the newspaper appeared on June 28. *BOILING AGAIN: There was another submarine explosion on the bay yesterday east of the GR&I depot. The water was thrown in the air about 20 feet and the commotion was vigorous and continued several minutes . . . . This is the third eruption of this kind this season.*

Various theories were offered as the story made its way around town. Some were serious, some capricious, but none seemed to fit. And apparently the phenomenon was never seen again—at least, none was ever again reported by the newspaper. It remained a mystery.

The most logical explanation came recently from a specialist in the science of hydrology. He says that the eruptions were probably caused by the seepage of natural gas from a layer of broken shale below the lake bed. Over time it collected in pockets in the soft, porous limestone layer above, and when the pressure reached a certain level it blew up.

TRAGEDY IN THE U.P.

Back in the late 1880s and early 1900s many Michigan deer hunters traveled north to the Upper Peninsula to do their hunting. In those days, if you wanted a better than even chance of getting a deer, that was the place to go.

That was because deer were scarce in lower Michigan. Seventy-five years of what amounted to clear-cut logging of the great forests had raised hob with deer habitat. That, together with unrestricted hunting, had almost wiped out the herd. In the 1900s, Michigan's deer population was estimated at a mere 50,000. Compared with around 3.2 million white-tails today, that was getting dangerously close to extinction.

On November 2, 1898, Judge Roscoe L. Corbett and his 17-year-old son Charles left Traverse City on the train to their hunting camp at Ozark, near Trout Lake Junction. They spent a few days putting the camp in order before they were joined by other members of the group, including Corbett's best friend, David Kuhns, and Dr. A. J. DeLacy.

On the afternoon of November 7, 1898, at the start of the deer hunting season, Corbett and his son were walking with loaded guns in the woods near the camp when suddenly a shot rang out. The Judge cried, "I'm killed!" and fell to the ground, mortally wounded. Charles ran for help from other members of the party, and together they carried his father back to camp. Dr. DeLacy examined the injured man, and found that the wound was mortal—the bullet had entered Corbett's back and exited at the pit of his stomach. There was nothing anyone could do to save his life.

For two hours Kuhns sat beside the man's bed and tried to comfort him, while Corbett drifted in and out of consciousness. Then, about five o'clock, the Judge, opening his eyes, recognized his friend and indicated there was something he wanted to tell him. Putting his arm around Kuhns' neck, he drew him down close to his lips.

"Goodbye, old friend," he whispered in his ear, and died.

A short time after the accident Charles said that he thought he had seen a hunter sitting on a stump back in the woods and a deer on the opposite side of the road, but he wasn't sure. One of the hunters made a wide circle through the woods around the spot where Corbett fell, but found no human tracks. All were convinced that it must have been a stray bullet, fired at some distance away.

Corbett's body, in a plain pine box obtained at Trout Lake Junction, was accompanied on the train back to Traverse City, by his son and other members of the party. In order to avoid an 8-hour layover at Walton Junction, a special train was dispatched from Traverse City to bring them and the body home.

At first, son Charles came under suspicion that it was he who, accidentally or otherwise, fired the fatal shot. This was completely disproved by the autopsy, which revealed that Corbett had been shot by a rifle bullet, while everyone knew that Charles was carrying a shotgun loaded with buckshot. Corbett's gun, undischarged, was lying on the ground where he fell.

Nevertheless, a small cloud of suspicion hung over the young man's innocent head for many years—until 1915, in fact, when a man in Alpena confessed on his deathbed that he had accidentally fired the shot.

TORNADO

All Hell—or something awfully close to it—broke loose in the Grand Traverse region on the evening of April 3, 1956.

A tornado tore through three counties in less than one hour, touching earth at least six times and leaving one dead, 19 injured, and damage estimated at more than a million dollars. It was all the more terrifying because only a few people in the area had ever seen a tornado before.

It came off Lake Michigan near Bear Lake with a pent up fury like the wrath of God and touched down first at Thompsonville, where it took the life of Mrs. Hugh Parks, 85, and critically injured her husband. Mrs. Parks was killed when her home collapsed around her. Also injured were Mrs. Edna Beechraft and her two-year-old son Ricky; and Mrs. Nellie Kast. It leveled several other homes, completely destroyed Homestead Community Church, and uprooted big trees.

The twister struck next at Honor, where several people jumped into a well pit at the home of Robert Rhodes, as the gale ripped off the roof of his house. Several other homes were damaged.

Next to bear the tornado's wrath was Lake Ann. There it destroyed the home of Mrs. Lillian Gray, who suffered multiple injuries. Other houses were damaged, and a car was smashed when the cement block walls of its garage fell in on it.

The deadly funnel cloud lifted into the sky again but came to ground a scant three miles north at the tiny community of Cedar Run, eight miles west of Traverse City. There it flattened half the village and injured 13 people, seven of whom were taken to the hospital.

Three families, all inter-related and living in adjacent houses, were especially hard hit.

The Courtad family—Richard and Maxine and their children, Douglas, 9, Carol Ann, 5, and Mary Jo, 4—all were outdoors when the tornado hit. All suffered cuts and bruises from flying debris (all except Richard, who was headed for town but turned around when he saw the storm cloud and arrived back home after it had passed). But the two little girls were missing. They were found by the faithful family dog, a collie named "Collie", and pulled from the debris. Collie won several awards for heroic conduct.

Courtad had a regular job in town, but raised mink as a sideline. The storm wrought havoc with the mink yard, scattering mink and cages about and killing many of the animals. Dick had help the next day from fellow mink ranchers in rounding up the live animals running around all over the place.

Joel and Vivian Loomis (Joel and Maxine Courtad were brother and sister) and their children, Bobby, 8, Judy, 4, Virginia, 3, and Darlene, 8 months, were in their house nearby when it exploded around them. All of the Loomises sustained multiple cuts and bruises, and when they counted noses they discovered that baby Darlene was missing. She was found, after a frantic search, in a small swamp behind the house. She was lying under the kitchen stove, which was holding up an uprooted tree. Miraculously, the baby suffered only a cut on her forehead, the faint scar of which she still bears.

Also injured were Marion and Sadie Loomis, Joel's parents, who survived. They operated a small store and until 1934 a post office in their house, which the tornado totally destroyed.

The twister went on to inflict serious damage at Solon, Keswick, and Suttons Bay, and then dissipated over West Grand Traverse Bay.

THE FRENCHMAN AT FOUNTAIN POINT

An aura of mystery still clings to a French fur trader miscalled Aymer Belloy.

In New York, in 1854, the Frenchman hired sea captain Cassimer Boischer to sail his (Belloy's) schooner *Oglebay* to the Great Lakes via the Erie Canal. The two men spent the summer together, trading with the Indians at Green Bay and Grand Traverse Bay. The trip included an extended stay at Peshawbestown, where Belloy hired two Indian guides for an exploratory expedition around Carp Lake (now Lake Leelanau).

On their way back to Detroit in the fall of that year they stopped at the new land office at Duncan City near Cheboygan, where both men bought land, Boischer in Suttons Bay and Belloy in the Carp Lake area. In 1855 they sailed to New York, where Belloy bought well-drilling equipment and delivered it to Leland aboard the *Oglebay*. Belloy stayed with the Boischers that winter, and in the spring of 1856 they shook hands and parted at Buffalo, Boischer having bought the *Oglebay*.

In 1867 Belloy formed a company known as Grand Traverse Mineral Association, and some of the mystery about him began to clear. It turned out that his real name was Marquis Aymer de Belloi. He was an aristocrat, born to a prominent Parisian family. Rumor had it that, because of his involvement in some kind of scandal, he had been banished by the family to exile in America. Perhaps he was what was called a "remittance man", supported by the family but forever barred from returning to his native land.

In any case, in 1867—eight years after the first successful oil well was drilled in Pennsylvania—de Belloi started drilling for oil on the east side of the Carp Lake Narrows about a mile south of the tiny village of Provemont (Lake Leelanau). On April 28, 1867, the *Grand Traverse Herald* ran the following news item: "The Grand Traverse Mining Company have resumed their operations at their well on Carp Lake (near A. D. Belloy's) and intend to prosecute the work vigorously this summer."

The company continued its drilling, and at about 700 feet it hit a gusher—not of oil but of artesian water. The book, *Traverse Region of 1884* summed it up as follows: "In 1867, the Grand Traverse Bay Mineral Land Association sunk a well, expecting to strike oil, but failed of their object. There is, however, an artesian well of some 700 feet deep, from which spouts a stream of mineral water about six inches in diameter, rising to a height of twelve or fifteen feet. This water possesses valuable medicinal qualities."

And it's still going strong.

So is Fountain Point summer resort. In 1890 a man named L. C. Morrison bought the property and built a small hotel, which later he enlarged to 40 rooms and a central dining room. It is now one of the oldest on-going resorts in northern Michigan, and is listed as such in the Michigan Register of Historic Places and was nominated recently for the National Register.

What happened to the Marquis? Nobody seems to know. One rumor is that, crushed by his failure to find oil and by the bankruptcy of his company, he went back to New York and committed suicide.

FUNNY MONEY IN 1933

On the black day of November 13, 1929, the New York Stock Exchange took a dive that sent shock waves all over the country. It ushered in the Great Depression, which lasted more than a decade and might have lasted longer if it hadn't been for the Second World War. In 1933, to save American banks, President Franklin D. Roosevelt declared a "One Hundred Day Bank Moratorium", March 9 to June 16.

Nobody had any money, and jobs were almost impossible to find. In Traverse City, in 1933, some 500 able-bodied workers were without a job. In March of that year, a group of civic leaders, including Arnell Engstrom and Will Hardy, got together and worked out a plan to help the unemployed and give business a booster shot.

The gist of it was that the city itself hire the unemployed for work on civic projects that needed to be done. Things like cleaning up the river and brushing out its banks. Things not necessarily urgent, but nevertheless beneficial to the whole community.

The city commission liked the plan but asked what would they use for money? The answer was "script", a substitute for money. It would be self-liquidating and used for a finite length of time (one year) to purchase goods and services from participating merchants. One these terms, the City Commission enthusiastically endorsed the plan and lost no time in implementing it.

Here's how it worked. The City printed 2,000 pieces of script in denominations of one dollar and one half-dollar. Certificates all had 52 squares on the back for pasting in two- or one-penny stamps purchased in advance by all merchants honoring the script. Each transaction had to be accompanied by a stamp, dated and initialed. The script had to change hands at least once a week. Thus, after 52 transactions, the City Treasurer had one dollar (or one half-dollar) in hand to redeem the certificates in cash, plus four cents to pay for the printing. Workers were paid $2 per day in script for a nine-hour day. Most of the merchants signed up.

On March 15, the first 32 workers began the work of cleaning up the banks of the Boardman River. Brush, tin cans, old wagons, and other rubbish was gathered up and tossed into bonfires along the riverbanks, and the remainder hauled away.

A week later, City Engineer C. E. Sawyer opened the Union Street dam, lowering the depth of the pond above, and another crew began removing stumps, deadheads, and other debris between Cass and Eighth Street bridges.

(One thing they didn't find was a Napolean automobile, said to have been driven into the river by a car thief, and never recovered.)

Later the dam was closed, and the crew started work on the lower part of the river, for the first time in its history, removing the trash that had accumulated over the many years that the City had used the river as a dumping place and for sewage disposal.

Other much needed work included such tasks as widening and ditching Front Street from Union and East Bay, rebuilding the river wall along the Manistee & Northeastern property just west of the North Union Street bridge, building roads in Clinch Park, cutting down trees at the City gravel pit and buzzing 400 cords of wood to be passed out to needy families, and cleaning Asylum Creek and the beach between Clinch Park and the Wequetong Club. Altogether, more than 150 workers were involved. The script ran out in early April and the City printed 2,000 more certificates. Some of this went to paying school teachers' salaries.

In the end, most people agreed that the project had been a success. It didn't cost the City one red cent. The merchants made out well enough. And, best of all, it put some money in the pockets of those who needed it most.

TRAGEDY AT THE FAIR

Her name was Deborah de Costello. She was a pretty little Spanish girl in her twenties who jumped out of airplanes. People paid to see her jump out of airplanes. She barnstormed the country with her pilot and mechanic, Charley Radcliffe, in a two-seater biplane named Ethel Dare, putting on parachute-jumping exhibitions at small town carnivals and county fairs. She was famous as the one and only female parachutist in the world.

In 1920, Deborah was scheduled to make several jumps for a fee of $1,000 at the week-long Fair at Empire, beginning on September 23. She and Charley Radcliffe arrived on Friday, the first day of the Fair, landing on an open field near the fairgrounds. A crowd quickly gathered around the plane, pressing close to shake her hand and ask for autographs. Many of them had never seen an airplane, at least not up that close. They marveled at how such a pretty, warm, and vulnerable-looking little girl could have the nerve to make parachute jumps. Meanwhile, Charley wandered off, stooping now and then to pinch off blades of grass and toss them in the air to gauge the wind.

Deborah's first jump was scheduled for that afternoon, but by that time the weather had changed abruptly—with strong northwest winds and rain squalls—and it had to be cancelled. The weather was even worse on Saturday and Sunday. Attempts were made on Monday and Tuesday, but Charley wasn't satisfied with weather conditions, and refused to let Deborah jump, even though she was willing. The weather was also bad on Wednesday and Thursday, and the Fair officials met with Debbie and offered her $400 for expenses, exhibition or no exhibition, but she insisted on fulfilling her contract. The weather forecast for Friday looked favorable, and two jumps were scheduled, one at Empire and one at Honor.

Friday's weather was perfect, with a light breeze off the water and hardly a cloud in the sky. As scheduled, the plane took off to the cheers of the crowd. Charley circled several times above the field to gain altitude, then leveled out. The crowd could barely see Deborah as she climbed out on the wing and jumped, but all could see the parachute, opening like a flower, with the tiny figure dangling below it.

But then a terrible thing happened. The wind suddenly shifted from west to east, and instead of falling straight down, the parachute began to drift out over the water. Charley saw it immediately and circled back. Desperately he tried three times to hook the parachute with the wings of the plane, but failed. As he tried for the fourth time, Deborah and the chute disappeared into the waters of Lake Michigan.

The Sleeping Bear Coast Guard spent two days searching for her body. But it wasn't until weeks later that a man walking the beaches found it under one of the Empire Lumber Company docks. She was buried at Empire in St. Philip's Church cemetery. Her simple gravestone bears only her name and the dates: Deborah de Costello, 1893-1920.

THE ROEN MYSTERY

On a stormy midsummer night in 1977, Severt Roen, 75, walked out the door of the farmhouse near Empire where he lived with his two brothers, Andrew and Benhart, and never came back. He was never seen or heard from again.

The three brothers were sons of Norwegian immigrants Andrew, Sr., and Randi, who came to Empire in 1892. They were said to be among the first families to settle in Norway Town, a community of Norwegian sawmill workers on the south side of town. The senior Roen got a job stacking lumber at the Empire Lumber Company.

When the mill closed down he bought a 133-acre fruit farm near Empire and raised five sons there: Gilbert, Alfred, Benhart, Severt, and Andrew, Jr. At about the same time he bought a saloon on Niagara Street and ran it until Prohibition put him out of business. He died in 1946.

After their father's death the five sons took over the operation of the farm. But Gilbert and Alfred soon got married and left the farm to the other three. Those three never married and only one, Ben, ever had a girl friend. They became more and more reclusive as the years went by, evidently satisfied with their own company.

The trouble started many years later, when Severt began to show signs of senility. His brothers were sympathetic at first but as time went by and his condition worsened, they found it hard to cope with him.

Dave Taghon, one of the brothers' few friends, remembers taking Severt home when he found him wandering about town.

"I knocked on the door and when Ben opened it and saw Severt standing there, the sound of his voice went right through me. He loudly told him to get back to the orchard. Severt was shaking. It was obvious they didn't show much respect for poor old Severt."

Afterward, most people believed that it was his brothers' harsh treatment that drove Severt to leave home for good.

For three months, search parties including Boy Scouts and officers of the law scoured the countryside fruitlessly for some trace of the missing man. A self-styled psychic named Hilda Joy suggested that Severt's body might be found in the cistern, an underground water tank on the farm. The authorities checked it out but found the tank empty and dry. Other theories of foul play gave rise to rumors that Severt was buried in a new garden bed or in a new septic system for an additional bathroom that was never hooked up, or behind a seemingly fresh patch of cement on a basement wall. But the authorities dismissed these notions as frivolous.

County coroner Dr. Matthew Houghton, who was also the Roen brothers' personal physician, said Andy told him he believed that Severt had hitched a ride on the highway and was still alive.

"For all we know," Gary Hilts, another friend of the brothers, said, "he could have gone downstate and died a pauper."

It was Hilts and Dave Taghon who found the two remaining brothers—Andy, 75, and Ben, 87—dead at the farmhouse on the morning of January 17, 1985. Hilts, who knew their habits, had made several calls to the house but nobody answered and he sensed that something was wrong.

They found Ben on the parlor floor, perhaps having fallen off the couch, and Andy dead in bed; he was a diabetic and Ben took good care of him. Both had died of natural causes, the coroner said. He estimated that Andy had been dead for a week, Ben not more than two or three days. Dave Taghon believes that Ben lost his will to live after Andy died.

Hilts and Taghon were appointed by Empire Bank to take inventory. The brothers weren't exactly misers, but they hated to spend a nickel on anything they didn't need; and rumors had been flying that there must be bags of money stashed all over the house. Hilts and Taghon did find one bag containing $20,000 in cash in a filing cabinet, but most of it was in Social Security envelopes in another cabinet.

"We found more than $100,000 in cash in just the first hour of the first day," Taghon said.

The brothers kept a careful record of all money received and money spent. Their ledgers included such insignificant items as 25 cents found in their mother's bureau after she died; money found under Sievert's bed after he left; and the purchase of two ice cream cones at a downtown drive-in.

The inventory, filed at Probate Court, included bank accounts, real estate, antiques, vehicles, and contents of the house. The whole estate was appraised at $450,000.

A public auction of the Roen family heirlooms was held at the farm on Labor Day of 1985. It drew 5,000 buyers from 23 states and two Canadian provinces. Some of the big ticket items included a Dewey twin floor slot machine for $18,500, a Judge slot machine that sold for $8,500, and a jukebox with metal discs that brought $5,000. The Empire Area Heritage Group bought the magnificent mahogany bar and the fixtures of the old Roen Saloon for $5,000. They also bought for $1,200 a wooden model two-masted schooner, made by a Norwegian immigrant; it had adorned the Roen bar in the old days.

All these items are on permanent display at the Heritage Group's headquarters in downtown Empire.

ATTEMPTED MURDER

The tiny village of Traverse City had hardly recovered from the shock of its first murder case in 1861 when, a year later, on the Fourth of July, an attempt was made to kill one of Traverse City's most prominent citizens, James K. Gunton.

Gunton was one of the city's earliest pioneers. He came here in 1851 and for several years worked as a carpenter for Hannah, Lay & Company. Later he built one of the earliest hotels, the Gunton House, on the corner of Front and Wellington Streets. A big, balding, jovial man with a drooping mustache, he and his wife made the Gunton House one of the most popular hospitality places in town.

E. F. French was a newcomer. He and his wife had come to town a few weeks previously from Greenville, Michigan, where he had been engaged in a highly successful real estate business—or so he said. He planned to open a land agency here, too, he said. Shortly after their arrival the couple had lost a baby, born and buried here.

On the afternoon of the Fourth, French was at the Gunton House, drinking ale with other celebrants of the national holiday. He seemed to be in good spirits (both literally and figuratively), but as the day wore on he became noisier and more quarrelsome. His wife called at the House in the evening and tried to persuade him to come home, but he brushed her off with abusive language. At this point Gunton himself came around the bar and asked French to leave. Sharp words followed, but finally French left, threatening to come back and "attend to Mr. Gunton's case."

French went home and took down a double-barrel shotgun. He told his wife that he was going to kill Gunton for insulting him. She implored him not to, and began to scream—her screams were heard at the Gunton House nearby. Two or three men came running and found French with the gun in his hands, threatening to kill Gunton before morning. After talking with them for a while, French promised to postpone the execution until morning, and the men left, satisfied that he would come to his senses by that time. Nevertheless, they warned Gunton to keep a sharp lookout.

As soon as they were gone, French instructed his wife to sell the furniture, disinter the body of her child, take it back to Greenville for reburial, and take herself to her parents at Grand Haven. He also told his wife that if she put up any resistance, her would shoot her on the spot. Then he loaded the gun with slugs and returned to the Gunton House.

There he went around to a barroom window, took careful aim, and fired both barrels at Gunton, who was standing behind the bar. One of the rounds struck a glass pitcher and a glass dish on the bar and shattered them into a thousand pieces. The other hit Gunton on the arm, inflicting only a slight wound. Witnesses said later that if it hadn't been for the intervening glass objects, Gunton would have been a dead man.

French then took to the woods, armed with a rifle, revolver, and bowie knife. He was seen at four o'clock next morning on horseback seven miles south of town on the old Indian trail to Saginaw. The Sheriff and Gunton had already ridden off in pursuit but never did catch up with him. And, as far as Traverse City knew, he was never seen or heard from again.

THE DAY THE DAMS BROKE

It rained Tuesday. It rained Wednesday. It also rained hard on Thursday. Altogether, almost seven inches of rain fell on the Traverse City area in one sixty hour period, September 12-14, 1961. Something had to give.

In 1961 there were four hydroelectric dams on the Boardman River. In chronological order they were: the Boardman River Dam, built in 1894; the Sabin Dam, 1907; the Keystone Dam, 1909; and the Brown Bridge Dam, 1921. In addition, there was a power dam at Mayfield on Swainston Creek, which flows into the Boardman River; it supplied power to Mayfield and Kingsley.

It was the first to go.

The Mayfield Dam held out until early morning, September 14, then broke under the force of pent-up water and washed out with a roar that awoke the sleeping villagers. A ten-foot wall of water rushed down the creek, clearing everything in its path, and joined the already swollen Boardman River at its outlet a mile or so downstream from Brown Bridge Dam. From there it swept downriver like a tidal wave, washing out a mile and a half of River Road, stranding vehicles and flooding many cottages along the way.

That was too much for Keystone Dam, already at a critical stage.

Actually, Keystone Dam consisted of two dams—one for the power plant and one for a holding pond. When it was built, the river was diverted to a new channel several hundred feet to the east and a concrete wall for the holding pond and spillway were built parallel to the channel. When the flood waters arrived, they spilled over the holding pond dam and quickly undermined and washed it out. The river reverted to its original course and left the power dam high and dry.

The floodwaters were contained in the Boardman Dam pond, and it and the Sabin Dam suffered no damage.

Upriver, though, was another story. A logjam and other debris at the Pennsylvania Railroad bridge dammed the river and threatened River Road and cottages with further damage. Volunteers came from everywhere to help. Crews from the county sheriff's department and from Grawn worked hours that night clearing the jam. They lowered men on ropes who attached lines to the logs and other rubbish and hauled them out of the river. This hazardous work was completed without accident except for dunking Sid Russell of Grawn when a knot came loose. He was quickly hauled to safety.

Keystone Dam was never rebuilt and now only remnants of it remain. Sabin, Boardman, and Brown Bridge dams are still in operation.

YEAR OF THE GRASSHOPPER

At first it was just a trickle. But then it grew into a swarm, then a cloud, then a horde, and finally, a plague. Grasshoppers by the millions. In the fields and even in the streets. Grasshoppers everywhere. The local farmers, most of them, called them a calamity.

Plagues of locusts go back at least to Biblical times, but so far as Traverse City people were concerned, the great 1920 plague of locusts (commonly called grasshoppers) was the grand-daddy of them all.

According to word from the south on Saturday morning, July 10, great swarms of grasshoppers had reached Wexford and were heading north. They arrived at Buckley a short time later. By noon they had descended on Traverse City by the millions and were still coming.

Residents on Washington Street said they were so thick that night hawks came out to feed on them. On Sunday morning, downtown sidewalks were so covered with the pests that it was almost impossible to walk without crunching a bunch of the nasty little critters underfoot. On the Ott property and other vacant lots they were thick as morning dewdrops, and they rose in clouds when people walked across them. Many people complained that the hoppers were eating up their gardens.

In the meantime, some Grand Traverse County farmers had declared war on the hoppers. Their only weapon in those days was a poison recommended by agricultural agent Robert A. Wiley— a mixture of white arsenic, salt, molasses, and fine sawdust to be spread on the fields while still damp. He said that grasshoppers were attracted to the molasses—they loved sweets.

With agent Wiley's assistance, a few of the townships in the county organized mixing stations, paid for by the township boards. The farmers drove up to the station and filled their wagons with the mixture, drove home, and applied it according to the agent's directions.

Did the poison kill the grasshoppers?

It sure did.

In late June, Wiley paid a visit to one of Grant Township's farmers. He waned to see with his own eyes how effective the mixture had been on the hopper horde. Even Wiley was a bit surprised.

Most of the Grant Township farmer's crop was corn. Every furrow made by the cultivator between the rows of corn was filled with dead hoppers. Even the imprint of the horse's hooves was full of them. Just for exhibition purposes, Wiley took them from one hoof track and counted 237. The collection was put on display at the Chamber of Commerce window.

In August, Wiley estimated that even though the poison did a pretty good job, the damage to the crops was ten times as bad as in 1918 and 1919.

"I can name a hundred farmers in this area whose crops have been almost totally destroyed," Wiley said. "There were just too many grasshoppers."

THE CASE OF THE GERMAN BANKNOTE

In the immediate aftermath of World War I, Germany was gripped in the throes of an economic collapse. Its paper currency, the Reichsmark—roughly equivalent to the U. S. dollar—was worth practically nothing. In 1923, for example, it took hundreds, even thousands, of marks to buy a package of cigarettes.

On September 17, 1976, a young man named Stephen Holcomb, Jr., walked into Traverse City's National Bank & Trust with a 1923 100,000 Reischsmark bank note and asked one of the tellers to cash it for whatever it was worth. After consulting on the telephone with one of the bank's officers, who checked with a bank in Detroit, the teller paid Holcomb $39,700 in cash, which was the current value of the Reichsbank note. Holcomb thanked her kindly and walked out, a whole lot richer than when he walked in.

Within a day or two, NBT discovered its mistake and wanted its money back.

A few days later, the *Record Eagle* ran the story on Page One. It reported that the bank had already recovered all but $18,000 of its money and expected more soon. It had already commenced legal action to recover the remainder. Holcomb had stated that he did not try to defraud the bank. The newspaper story also included an interview with his mother, Helen Holcomb.

"Those bills have been knocking around the house for years," she said. "There must be 40 of them, and if they could all be cashed in at the rate my son got, they'd be worth $1.5 million."

She said she couldn't remember where or when she came into possession of the old German "inflation money."

"It's a big mess," she said. "Steve goes down to the bank, and they give him money."

She said her son had paid some bills and paid for some other things too, with the money.

But how could the bank make such a gross mistake?

"Given the right circumstances, anything is possible," a former NBT bank employee said. "Remember that the transaction took place around noon, and only one of our bank officials was on duty. The teller was an 18-year-old girl without much experience. She calls the official and tells him about the problem. He asks her what is the man's name, and she tells him Mr. Holcomb. Well, that's okay, he says, thinking it's Steve Holcomb, Sr., a well known, successful builder around town. 'Take care of him,' he says."

The *Record Eagle* story was only a column long, and it never had a follow-up. Apparently, it had no legs. Over the years, though, it developed some artificial ones. Tall tales are still being told about the affair—like the one that has Holcomb buying an expensive car, heading south and west, and spending money like a drunken sailor along the way—all without a shred of truth.

Oh, well. Why let truth spoil a good story?

EARTHQUAKE IN TRAVERSE CITY

On February 28, 1925, a strange phenomenon threw a scare into a lot of Traverse City people. At precisely 8:27 on a Saturday evening, it set dishes rattling, lamps swinging, rocking chairs rocking, and buildings swaying. Some people thought it was some kind of explosion, but it made no sound. A few, feeling the earth trembling under their feet, feared it signaled the end of the world.

As earth tremors go, it was trivial, lasting only a fraction of a second. But it was the first one ever experienced in Traverse City, and, indeed, the first one recorded in the whole of Michigan.

Except for a handful of people who had spent some time in California—where earthquake vibrations are commonplace—no sooner had the tremor stopped than telephones started ringing as neighbor called neighbor to find what it was all about.

Fledgling radio broadcast stations were first to break the news to the few people who had a radio, and on Monday the *Record-Eagle* ran detailed stories on the front page under the banner headline EARTHQUAKE HERE FIRST EVER FELT. The newspaper reported, perhaps with tongue-in-cheek, that at least 500 local people were sure they were going to have a stroke. At least 500 more decided to quit smoking. Perhaps some more even swore off drinking hooch.

Up at the Elks Club seven men were playing poker. Six of them were smoking cigars. As the building started rocking and the table became unsteady, every one of the six stubbed out his cigar, convinced that he was smoking too much for his own welfare.

The *Record Eagle* also ran a United Press release quoting earthquake expert Dr. Chester A. Reed of the American Museum of Natural History that the slipping of a rock mass in the Atlantic Ocean off the coast of Maine caused the earth tremor of Saturday night which shook the entire northeastern part of the United States and eastern Canada, and was felt as far west as Wisconsin.

Dr. Reed said that the evidence indicated the quake was due to a fault or fracture of the ocean bed extending from the Bay of Fundy southward to the Isle of Shoals, off Portsmouth, N. H. This fracture, known as the Fundian Fault, had been dormant a long time, but there was evidence that it was responsible for severe New England earthquakes during the 17th and 18th centuries.

1296 1681 1600 1444

HARTS CAMP

TIMBER!

THE OLD BOARDMAN SAWMILL

From its mouth at Boardman Lake, the Boardman River flows northwesterly across Traverse City to Wadsworth Street, a little south of Front Street. Here it does a 180-degree turn to the east, flowing parallel to the West Bay shore, and empties into Grand Traverse Bay at a point almost exactly north from its emergence at Boardman Lake. The two points are only about half a mile apart.

Kid's Creek (first called Mill Creek, then Asylum Creek) meets the Boardman River at its western most bend at Wadsworth Street. With its three or four main tributaries, this creek drains the hills southwest of Traverse City. It flows north through the State Asylum grounds, and the 1851 plat map shows that a good part of the grounds along Elmwood Street was covered by a small lake. It was created by backwater from the old Boardman sawmill, and formed a mill pond for logs headed for the mill. People ice-skated on this pond in the winter.

Construction of the old Boardman sawmill stemmed from the 1847 purchase of 200 acres of virgin pine timberlands at the foot of Grand Traverse Bay by Harry Boardman, a well-to-do farmer from Naperville, Illinois. Boardman sent his son Horace and two or three hired men to make plans for a sawmill and they arrived at the site in June of 1847, setting immediately to work on a rude dwelling, sixteen feet by twenty-four, of pine logs hewn square with broadaxes. In later years this structure was known as the "Old Blockhouse." It burned down in 1878.

Horace intended to dam the Boardman River there and build the mill near the Blockhouse, but then changed his mind and decided to build a larger mill on the stream he named Mill Creek. This was a much easier undertaking, and he could use the lumber from the small mill to build the larger one.

Meanwhile, Harry Boardman had sent a crew of carpenters and engineers from Chicago to assist in the work and together with all the white men and Indians at Rev. Peter Dougherty's mission on Old Mission Peninsula, they finished raising the mill and got it into operation about the first of October. The first boards were used to finish the Blockhouse.

The mill hands had a long walk from the Blockhouse to the bigger mill on Mill Creek. The path between the two was on the southwest bank of the river, and the men had to cross it on a makeshift bridge of poles. Later, a more substantial bridge was built to carry wagons across.

In the summer of 1848, Boardman built a dock on the bay and a wooden-rail tramway between it and the mill. Lumber from the mill was carried to the dock on horse- or mule-drawn flatcars for shipment to Chicago on the schooner *Arrow*. The modest mill with its single muley saw continued in operation until Perry Hannah and his partners bought the property in 1851 and built a much larger steam mill on the bay on the present-day site of Clinch Park.

The 1851 U. S. Government Re-Survey (the first survey in 1840 was done so poorly it had to be done all over again in 1851) shows how the tiny Traverse City settlement looked when it was only three years old. The Old Blockhouse is shown clearly and so is the bridge across the Boardman River and the path to the sawmill, identified as "wagon trail." It also shows and identifies the Boardman sawmill, the tramway (identified as "railroad") and the dock on Grand Traverse Bay. Also shown in the long narrow millpond on the Asylum grounds.

In terms of today's landmarks, after flowing north past the Asylum, Kid's Creek passes under West Front Street at Ace Hardware, then makes an elbow bend to the east. It then flows under Division Street through a concrete tunnel just north of Front Street and runs fast between high steep banks not more than 30 feet apart; the river itself varies from 12 to 15 feet wide. Here, about 50 yards east of Division Street, was the ideal place for a dam.

The sawmill stood on what is now a parking lot behind the old Farm Bureau Building at 124 North Division Street. Both mill and dam have vanished without a trace. Perry Hannah used the mill for a short time to cut lumber, then turned it into a flour mill. Later, in 1867, Joseph Greilick used it to manufacture doors, sash, flooring and molding, but the old mill was abandoned when he built a large factory at the foot of Division Street in 1879. Both mill and dam were torn down shortly thereafter.

THE LAST BIG LOGGING

The last big logging in this area was on North Manitou Island. In 1908 two Traverse City men, W. Cary Hull and Frank Smith, bought a large tract of hardwood timber on the island. Their firm was known as Smith & Hull Lumber Company. Hull was the son of Henry Hull, founder and president of the Oval Wood Dish Company, one of Traverse City's largest industries; Smith was a landlooker, or timber cruiser, for that company.

That same year they built a sawmill at the already established village of Crescent on the west side of the island, and five miles of narrow-gauge railroad. In 1909 the company began operations on a big scale, hauling its first load of logs with a second-hand Shay locomotive on July 12. In the fall of that year they bought a second, brand-new "sidewinder" from the Lima Locomotive & Machine Works, and built three more miles of track. The engine was shipped by rail to Frankfort, then transported to the island on a barge.

In a short time Crescent grew from a mere handful of people to a good-sized settlement with a population of about 300, a hotel, post office, school and saloon. For several years the mill was a beehive of activity, processing millions of board feet of lumber for shipment to Traverse City, Chicago and Detroit. It is said that ships made stops there averaging one a day at the company's 600-foot dock.

But the lumber ran out in 1915, and the mill closed down. On July 5 all the mill machinery was loaded aboard the schooner *J. L. Nessen* and she sailed away carrying almost everything that made the sawmill a sawmill and Crescent a town. The railroad's rolling stock and rails were removed sometime later.

A few people lingered for a while. But most of the residents moved to the settlement on the east side of the island, and to the mainland, and it wasn't long before the village was completely deserted.

Now all that's left is a big old barn built in 1925, the concrete foundations for the mill's steam engine, a few spiles of the dock, and miles of railroad grade running through the woods from nowhere to nowhere.

OLD LOGGING RAILROADS

Among the few vestiges of old logging days in the Grand Traverse Region are the miles and miles of abandoned logging railroads running from nowhere to nowhere. Only the railroad beds themselves remain; the rails and ties were taken up long ago. But the grades, many of them, are almost perfectly preserved, and it gives one a kind of queer feeling to come upon them unexpectedly in the deep woods, winding through the brush, the only sign of man's handiwork for miles around.

They make fine hiking trails if you don't care particularly where you're going. There are some good examples in the woods north of Indian Lake in the woods between Hobbs Highway and Rennie Lake Road. The railroad was built by Cobbs & Mitchell of Cadillac. They carried out extensive logging operations in the Boardman Valley, cutting the hardwoods after Perry Hannah had cut down the pines.

Other short-time railroad grades abound in the area around Pearl Lake. This timber was logged off around 1900 by the Wilce Company of Empire. They built a logging road known as the Empire & Southeastern Railroad, which connected with the Manistee & Northeastern at Empire Junction north of Honor, and had several short branches. Other railroads were built in the Kalkaska area by Louis Sands, one of the lumber kings of Manistee.

One of the last logging railroads to be built in this region was the Manitou Limited on North Manitou Island.

In 1908, two Traverse City men, W. Cary Hull and Frank H. Smith, bought a large tract of hardwood timber on the island. The firm was known as Smith & Hull Lumber Company. Hull was the son of Henry Hull, president of the Oval Wood Dish Company, one of Traverse City's largest industries. Smith was a land-looker or timber-cruiser for the same firm.

That same year they built a sawmill at the already established village of Crescent on the west side of the island, and five miles of logging railroad. In 1909 the company began operations on a big scale, hauling its first load of logs to the mill with a second-hand

Shay locomotive on July 12. In the fall of that year they bought a second "side-winder" from the Lima Locomotive & Machine Works, and built three more miles of track. The engine was shipped by rail to Frankfort, then transported to the island on a barge.

For the next several years the mill was a beehive of activity, processing millions of board feet of lumber for shipment to Chicago and Detroit on passing steamers. It is said that the ships, on both north and south passage, made stops averaging one a day at the company's 600-foot dock.

But the timber ran out and the mill closed down in 1917. Then it was dismantled and hauled away, as was the railroad rolling stock and rails. The town of Crescent that grew up around the mill has long since disappeared.

A VISIT TO THE PINERIES IN 1858

One crisp winter day almost 150 years ago, two Traverse City men paid a visit to the lumber camps amid the great pine forests along the Boardman River. They made the 40 mile round-trip in a sleigh drawn by two fast ponies. One of the men was Perry Hannah, the legendary lumberman who founded Traverse City and the other was Morgan Bates—life long friend of Horace Greeley—who came to Traverse City in 1858 to establish the region's first newspaper, the *Grand Traverse Herald*.

This was Bates' first visit to the lumber camps, and on February 18, 1859, he published an account of it in his newspaper. It was titled "A Visit to the Pineries". Here is his story in quotes and paraphrase:

"The first indication that we are in a lumber region is a large stable on our left, a small booth for the marker, a log rollway on our right, some 300 feet long, and a winding road down to the river."

At the foot of the hill was Canfield's shanty, but they passed it up because of the steep descent and drove a mile farther to Nelson's shanty on the opposite side of the river.

"Captain Nelson himself stood ready to take a line. The shanties are log houses fitted up with bunks, tables, benches, stoves, and all the conveniences for housekeeping. We dined sumptuously. The fare was first rate and the cooking excellent. Those who imagine that the lumbermen have a hard time of it in the woods are mistaken. They are well fed, well housed, well worked, and lead a jolly, free-and-easy life."

From Nelson's shanty they went on half a mile to Raney's camp.

"The log slide at this shanty is about 200 feet long and the descent to the river is very steep. The loaded teams came in from the woods and we were just in time to witness the descent of the logs to the river. After the logs are measured by the marker and the chains are loosed, they go thundering and crashing down the slope, plunged into the river, emerge again like a school of huge porpoises on a frolic at sea, throwing spray twenty feet into the air."

In one respect Bates was disappointed in the pineries.

"They did not present the somber and gloomy appearance that we expected."

He explained this by saying that much of the forest was Norway pine, which grows on an "open, sandy plain with little or no underbrush. The White pine is more scattered and of a much larger growth. We saw some logs three feet in diameter, all clear."

The pine forests, Bates wrote, were six miles on the north and south of the river and extended fifteen miles to the east on both banks. He praised the Hannah, Lay Company for its efficient operation and excellent record keeping.

Their business is so admirably systemized that they can tell at any time just how many logs they have in the river, how much lumber they will make, what they have cost, and at what time they will arrive at their mills in Traverse City. They have five shanties and employ about 100 men in the pineries. They will get out logs enough this winter to make about a million feet of lumber.

The two mills at Traverse City are competent to make 50,000 feet in 12 hours. They are situated on the narrow peninsula between the river and the bay. In the spring the logs are floated from the pineries directly to the rear of the mill, where they are hauled inside by machinery, converted into lumber, and placed upon the wharf in front ready to be loaded aboard vessels."

Bates was perhaps a bit too enthusiastic about the lumberjack's jolly, free and easy life; after all, he was hardly in any position to judge after making just one trip to the camps. By our standards, the work was hard and dangerous, and the pay was marginal. But he was right about the food. Most of the men ate very well indeed. Good food was their one luxury. Camps with good cooks were generally happy and productive. Others soon lost their workers or replaced their cooks.

CURIOSITIES

FLATTOP ON THE BAY

One foggy day in August of 1942, during the Second World War, a small number of people caught a glimpse of a strange creature on Grand Traverse Bay. Some thought it was a large boat lying low in the water, others that it resembled a submarine. Because of the fog nobody got a real good look at it except maybe an ex-Navy man who said it looked like an aircraft carrier, but much smaller than any he'd ever seen. And when no story appeared in the *Record-Eagle*, the rumor got around that it was a secret Navy project—a hush-hush affair.

The truth came out after the war. The strange critter was indeed an aircraft carrier. The Navy built two of them, the *Wolverine* and the *Sable*. They were known as "baby flattops." They were built expressly for training carrier pilots on the protected waters of Lake Michigan, where they were safe from prowling German U-boats off the eastern seaboard. They were less than half the size of a regular carrier, and their flight deck less than half as long. And because they had no need for a hangar deck—no need for airplane storage—they sat very low in the water. It was said that if you could land a fast plane on that thing, you could land one almost anywhere.

Both *Wolverine* and *Sable* were conversion vessels. They were converted from old paddlewheel passenger boats, stripped down and refitted at Buffalo, N.Y., in 1942 and 1943.

Wolverine left Buffalo on August 12, 1942, and headed for Chicago where, after a formal welcome by Mayor Kelly and other dignitaries, she began her training exercises. The trainees and the aircraft were based at Glenview Aircraft Station a few miles north of Chicago. (Her appearance on Grand Traverse Bay was probably occasioned by a need to seek shelter from a storm on her way to Chicago.)

Every morning at three o'clock, day in and day out, *Wolverine* left her anchorage on the Chicago waterfront and steamed north to land and launch the planes. When the wind was strong, she would radio Glenview to send the speedy Corsairs and Wildcat fighters. If the wind was moderate, the slower dive bombers and torpedo planes were called up. On rare days when no wind blew, the pilots were assigned to SNJ trainers. Each trainee had to make eight successful takeoffs and landings over a three-day period to qualify for advanced training on the regular carriers.

The best day for either carrier was on May 28, 1944, when *Sable* qualified 59 pilots in a single day with 488 landings in 531 minutes. It is estimated that a total of more than 20,000 trainees made the grade. Among them was George H. W. Bush, 41st President of the U. S., who was the second youngest man in the Navy to qualify.

Casualties among them were few. The carriers were always accompanied by small Coast Guard or Navy boats, ready and able to come quickly to the rescue of downed pilots. Planes were another matter. The lake bottom between Chicago and Milwaukee is littered with lost aircraft, not all of them the result of accidents. Without a hangar deck the carriers sometimes had to jettison planes over the side to make room for others to land. It's estimated that more than 300 naval aircraft lie on the lake bottom today.

A visit to Grand Traverse Bay by the *Sable* was documented and photographed. On March 10, 1943, she spent four hours on the Bay conducting an experiment with TDR drone planes taking off from Traverse City airport and landing on her deck. There were six of them. Four made successful landings; two of them splashed.

WHERE THE BUFFALO ROAM

It has been estimated that there were 40 million buffalo in America when the first white men arrived—the largest animal herd in history. Unlimited slaughter in the latter half of the 19th Century reduced their numbers almost to the point of extinction.

Now, however, thanks to the late Jerry Oleson--Traverse City grocery tycoon and philanthropist—and others, including the U. S. government, the buffalo are being raised in great numbers on federal lands and private ranches, and their future seems assured.

Oleson bought his original herd of twelve buffalo from a state park in Oklahoma in 1960. Now the herd numbers in the hundreds.

Their home on the range is a hilly 120 acres on U. S. 31, a mile or so south of Traverse City. There they have become a perennial tourist attraction, as well as a provider of buffalo meat for the Oleson markets. Buffalo meat is leaner than beef and contains less cholesterol.

A full grown bull stands six feet tall and weighs upwards of a ton. On a dead run it can hit a speed of 40 miles per hour. The cows are smaller but no less formidable.

"They are a dangerous animal," Oleson said. "You never know when they may take a notion to charge. I feel safer when there's a fence between them and me."

The buffalo herd is an absolute monarchy, ruled by one dominant male. He jealously guards his harem of all the cows. A few years ago, however, the Big Daddy of the Oleson herd was challenged by a younger bull and toppled from his throne. Now he is an outcast, not permitted even to eat with the rest of the herd, and wanders about like a lost soul. His bearded, sorrowful countenance bears a strong resemblance to that of James G. Blaine after his defeat for the presidency by Grover Cleveland in 1884, and suggests that he too might have been a candidate for the office if he had followed some other line of work.

The Oleson herd feeds on hay, grain, pasture grass, and discarded vegetables from the Oleson markets: buffalo will eat anything vegetative. The herd forages out-of-doors winter and summer. They live almost as long as people do; cows have a productive life of 40 years. Mating is in the fall, and single calves are born in the spring.

WHERE DID THE SAND COME FROM?

In the early 1920s Traverse City's waterfront was a mess. It was littered with the remnants of dead or dying factories, and cut off from the village by a network of railroad tracks. And it wasn't until 1926 that anything was done about it. That was when Con Foster, Floyd Clinch, and a few other visionaries started trying to convince their fellow citizens that Grand Traverse Bay had the potential of becoming Traverse City's most valuable economic asset.

After the city park was established in 1931—despite the opposition of a majority of the citizens and the Board of Commissioners, most of whom voted against it—the last stretch of beach to get cleaned up was along the Pennsylvania Railroad tracks on the narrow tongue of land between the Boardman River and the Bay. It was covered with cinders from the railroad, and with weeds, brush and trash, stretching from the east end of the park to the Wequetong Club, a distance of about a quarter mile.

In 1933, when John C. Rill, general manager of the Pennsylvania system, attended the National Cherry Festival, he was approached by Con Foster and other civic leaders who asked him for help in cleaning up the beach, and he was glad to comply. He left instructions with division railroad officials to help with the work. It consisted of clearing the beach of weeds, trimming the trees, and hauling ten carloads of pure beach sand all the way from Muskegon to cover up the cinders along the right of way and widen the beach. Then, for good measure, the railroad built a walk across the tracks near its depot on Park Street and down to the beach.

For several days that summer, men with horses, engaged by the railroad, were busy spreading the carloads of sand over the beach and the railroad right of way. The work finished just in time for the dedication of the Elsie Hannah Bathhouse. (It was removed in 1967.)

"Visitors at the dedication will see the best array of bathing beach equipment in the region," reported the *Traverse City Record Eagle*. "Diving platforms, rafts, slides, and a merry-go-round will be spotted on the beach and in the water. Along the shore will be a line of beach chairs and colored umbrellas."

Going all the way to Muskegon for beach sand for Traverse City seems like "carrying coals to Newcastle", but no doubt the Pennsy had good reason to do so.

WHY DIDN'T THEY RIDE HORSES?

This question was asked me years ago by a fourth grade pupil whose class I had given a talk about Perry Hannah. I told them that Hannah, "Father of Traverse City", was elected to the State legislature in 1855. To attend his first legislative session he traveled to Lansing in the dead of winter on snowshoes, accompanied by an Indian guide and a dog. They traveled an old Indian trail, and the snow was so deep that they could barely make fifteen miles a day. The trip took ten days.

It was a good question, and it had me stumped. I didn't know the answer, and I told the youngster so, saying that I would do some research on the subject and let him know, which I did.

The answer is that in the 1850s horses were scarce in Traverse City. Perry Hannah and a few other affluent people had buggy horses, but most of the farming and lumbering was done with oxen. An ox can do twice the work of a horse, and eats less. But oxen have two disadvantages: They're slow, and they can't back up.

In the 1850s horses in Traverse City were also very costly. In relative terms, a horse cost about as much as a small automobile does today.

It wasn't until the 1860s that entrepreneur Birney J. Morgan began importing horses to the Grand Traverse area. He bought them in Ohio and Indiana and shipped them to Traverse City by boat. Sometimes they were herded along the first State Road by his men. The Northport-Newaygo State Road was the first road north to the Grand Traverse region; it closely followed an ancient Indian trail and the present M-37. There were ferries across the big rivers—Grand, Muskegon, Pere Marquette, and Manistee—but the horses probably swam across with the herders riding bareback.

FIVE-CENT FLICKERS

Shortly after the turn of the century, a new form of entertainment began to capture enthusiasm here and abroad. Here they called it the movies; over there it was cinema. Here they also called it nickelodians and five-cent flickers because it cost only a nickel to get in. The old film speed was 16 frames per second, and on light scenes flickers on the screen were very noticeable. That's why early films were called flickers. The change from 16 to 35 frames per second corrected that problem. Another improvement was changing the screen from the canvas type to silvered.

Most of the early films were crude and unimaginative, but people flocked to them like bees to honey. Here was something new and different, almost mysterious. They couldn't get enough.

Motion pictures had several fathers, not just one. But it was Thomas Alva Edison who in 1898 devised the first true motion-picture equipment used in the United States.

The first American producer of dramatic films was Edwin S. Porter. He made the first films: "The Life of An American Fireman" and "Robinson Crusoe." His firm, Colonial Motion Picture Company, sold them all over the country, many to opera houses, including Steinberg's Grand Opera House and the City Opera House. On the evening of January 3, 1904, City Opera screened both films, the first in Traverse City. Admission was 25 and 35 cents for adults, 15 cents for children.

The first regular motion-picture theater in Traverse City was Dreamland, at 210 East Front Street. It was owned and operated by G. Lote Silver. It opened its doors somewhere around 1901. Behind its recessed entrance was a room for coin-operated phonographs of a cylinder type and you could listen to the music through rubber tubes. It also had a test-your-grip machine and others including a fortune-teller and a popcorn dispenser, but no candy.

The booth contained a Powers projector which had to be rewound by hand, and the booth itself was metal-lined to guard against fire. The floor of the theater was flat, which sometimes made it difficult to see the screen, but Silver later put in a sloped floor, which helped a lot. He usually had two vaudeville acts in addition to the films. Music was provided by a piano player. Many Charlie Chaplin one-reel comedies were shown. So was a series called "Musty Suffer Comedies."

The Palace Theater, at 128 East Front, opened in 1904 with three features: "Red Sweeney's Defeat", "Nellie's First Cake", and "Checkered Lives." On one of the billboards was a picture of a seated lady in a big hat staring over a checkerboard while a young man leans over her shoulder to make a move. Among other popular serials were "The Perils of Pauline" with Pearl White and "The Fatal Ring" with Warner Oland. The Palace showed mostly short subjects.

Another early moving picture theater was the Travis. It was located across the street from the Pacesetter Bank and wasn't around very long. The Lyric, the last of the flickers, was situated where the State Theater used to be. It burned down on January 17, 1923, and again on January 1, 1948.

Looking back, it was the motion picture theaters that did away with the opera houses, an estimated 2,000 of them nationwide. And now it appears that the movie theaters themselves are beginning to show signs of decline, threatened by home movies, DVDs and discs.

THE PASSENGER PIGEON IN MICHIGAN

"Men still live who, in their youth remember pigeons;
trees still live that, in their youth, were shaken by a living wind. But
a few decades hence only the oldest oaks will remember, and at long
last only the hills will know."
From a Monument to the Pigeon
Aldo Leopold, 1947

They came like a sudden storm, darkening the sky. Birds, millions and millions of birds, so many that they eclipsed the sun and filled the air with their cries, drowning out all other sound. It was the annual spring migration of the passenger pigeon from their winter quarters in the Gulf states from Texas to Florida.

As far as we know, the world had never seen anything like it, before or since.

To measure their vast numbers, the great ornithologist John James Audubon calculated that a flock of pigeons one mile wide—which was below average width—passing a given point at 60 miles per hour for three hours and allowing two birds per square yard would contain about 1,250,135,000 pigeons. And that was just one flock out of many.

The great spectacle was reported in the early 1600s by French explorers Cartier and Champlain. To the Pilgrims, the birds were a mixed blessing. In 1643, they descended on the Plymouth crops with voracity as to cause a serious threat of famine. Yet, five years later, when the crops failed, they saved the settlers from starvation.

In Michigan, they were an important source of food for both Indians and early white settlers. The passenger pigeon was a good size bird, somewhat larger than a mourning dove. The Indians preserved their flesh by drying and smoking it, the whites, by packing them in salt or by canning.

A heavily wooded area near Northport was a favorite nesting and feeding ground for the birds. William Joseph Thomas, pioneer at Northport, wrote about them in his history of the Thomas family.

"The first twelve years we were here, from 1856 to 1868, we used to see vast numbers of wild pigeons all through the warm season of the year. It was a grand sight in the spring and the sun was warm and bright, to go out about nine o'clock and watch the pigeons flying. The first appearance would not be large. But in a few days, the whole sky was alive with pigeons flying as close as they could fly. The flights would continue for one or two weeks."

Payson Wolfe, a direct descendant of a long list of Ottawa chiefs, was the champion pigeon hunter and shooter of the northland.

"Armed with his famous double-barrel, muzzle-loading shotgun and always accompanied by a number of his dozen children, he stood at the edge of the cliff-like hill," his daughter Etta wrote. "The children carried two big clothing baskets in which to gather the game. We frequently gathered upwards of 70 birds at one discharge of his gun. I have heard my mother say that once she saw him down

124 birds at one shot, and she was a truthful woman. Payson never went to breakfast until he bagged from 1,000 to 1,200 pigeons."

As railroad transportation to northern Michigan improved after 1870, professional hunters—so-called "pigeoners"—came from all over the country. Market hunters used trap nets. At one nesting site in Grand Traverse County in 1875, some 900 people were employed trapping live birds and killing "squabs" (young pigeons) for big city markets. The same year, at nesting sites in Newaygo, Oceana, and Grand Traverse counties, two million squabs were shipped to market. Another 2.4 million birds were trapped and shipped alive to shooting clubs all over the country.

Something had to give. As the flocks grew smaller and smaller with the passing years, people wondered what was happening. The last of the big flights in Northport took place in 1877, and in the following year at Petoskey. A few scattered flocks continued to appear, but their numbers grew smaller and smaller.

Who killed the passenger pigeon? What drove the species into extinction? The answer is still a subject of controversy. In any case, it isn't simple. Certainly the unregulated slaughter by commercial market hunters must take a large share of the blame.

But not all of it. It seems likely that with the loss of the great virgin forests—the habitat that fed, sheltered and protected the birds to some extent—their demise was inevitable sooner or later.

In any case, the last passenger pigeon died at the Cincinnati Zoological Garden on September 1, 1914.

THE DOG, THE OWL, AND THE INDIANS

Once upon a time, there lived a young man in upper New York State who yearned to become a preacher of the Gospel. His name was D. R. Latham. He studied theology at an eastern school and was licensed by the Methodist Episcopal church. There was an opening in Kansas, but Latham wanted to see the Great Lakes first thinking that otherwise he might never get to see them at all. Traveling by schooner, he stopped at Old Mission for a few days and was met with such a warm welcome from the early settlers that he consented to stay. He sent for his wife, who joined him in early October 1856. The Old Mission people hadn't seen a regular pastor since Peter Dougherty's removal to New Mission in 1852.

The other early settlements in the Grand Traverse area were in the same boat—including the small village of Traverse City (so small that you could bat a baseball from one end to the other.)

Latham began preaching and teaching regularly on June 21, 1857 in the church that Peter Dougherty had built. His circuit was Old Mission, Traverse City and later, Elk Rapids. In his early days, Latham taught school at Old Mission during the week, preached there on Sunday morning, walked to Traverse City and preached in the evening and then hiked back to Old Mission.

On the evening of March 14, 1858, Latham preached at Traverse City as usual, and then had refreshments at Perry Hannah's home on West Bay. To save time Latham planned to walk on the ice to Bowers Harbor, a distance of about eight miles. After lunch, he and Hannah went down to the beach together. Hannah cautioned him to stay away from the shore. In some places, he said, the ice had become dark, rotten, and dangerous. Latham thanked him and started out.

A thin crust of snow on the ice made the going good, and visibility was still adequate. A band of Indians was having a dance near the mouth of the Boardman River and Latham could hear the drums. Using the sound as a guide, he turned his back to it and kept going. But then after he had traveled about two miles a dense fog came down and visibility was reduced no more than a quarter mile.

He kept on, nevertheless, and after a long time he came upon Hog Island (now called Power Island). With Perry's advice in mind, he stayed away from shore and made a circuitous route around the island and into the harbor, hoping it would take him to Bowers home. In making the attempt, however, he lost his bearings and to make matters worse, the fog thickened cutting off all visibility. After traveling a long time and getting nowhere, he heard a dog barking and an owl hooting. They were welcome sounds, coming from the land and he headed in that direction.

Rain began to fall and the fog lifted. So did his spirits. Now he could see the darkened shore. But one obstacle remained. At a quarter mile from shore, the ice was black and rotten, extremely dangerous. Like most sensible people he began hollering for help. Answering shouts and guns firing from an Indian camp cheered him, and they guided him to the shore.

Latham thanked God for the dog and the owl and the Indians. Without them he might not have been able to tell his story.

THE STORY OF CAPTAIN JOE

His name was Cassimer Boischer, but among seafaring folk he was affectionately known as Captain Joe. Born in Three Rivers, Quebec, on January 25, 1827, he left home at the age of 14 and went to sea. By the time he turned 20, he was a qualified master of sailing ships. It was said that he was familiar with every port on the Great Lakes.

In 1854, he had just returned to New York from a trip around the Horn and back when he met a man named Aymer Belloy. Belloy was a French fur trader; he was looking for a skipper to sail his two-masted schooner, *Oglebay*, to the Great Lakes by way of the Erie Canal. Captain Joe took the job and spent the summer with Belloy trading with the Indians in the Grand Traverse and Green Bay areas.

The Captain fell in love with Grand Traverse Bay and resolved to make it his home some day. On their way back to Detroit at summer's end, he and Belloy stopped at the land office in Cheboygan and Cassimer bought 71 acres on the bay at what is now the town of Suttons Bay. The first patent or deed was issued on June 10, 1856, to Cassimer Boischer Dearwood and is recorded as Certificate No. 1, Vol. 1, Page 1. (Cassimer changed his name to Dearwood, which is the English translation of Boischer.) The Certificate was signed by Franklin Pierce, 14th President of the United States. They parted at Detroit, Captain Joe to winter there, Belloy to return to New York by rail.

At the Detroit Farmers Market, Cassimer met Pauline LaDuc—whom everybody called "Mother-crack-a-nut" because on every market day she would be in her booth selling cracked hickory nuts—and they became good friends. One day Cassimer said to her "Mother-crack-a-nut, I want to get married. Haven't you a daughter for me?"

"I have several," she said. "Come and see for yourself."

So Cassimer did come, and fall in love with sixteen-year-old pert and pretty Harriet with the dark brown hair and blue eyes; and within a month they were man and wife.

After a summer of sailing the *Oglebay* with Belloy, Captain Joe and his bride caught the last steamer to Mackinac Island, then hired a fishing boat to take them and their belongings to their homestead on Suttons Bay. There, in November of 1855, they built a log house with the help of an Ottawa Indian. Their only neighbors were the Tom Lees, a mile north, and the Sutton family, a mile south. And it was here that their first child Jane was born on August 28, 1856—the first white child born in the township. She was the first of nine children, eight girls and one boy.

Captain Joe bought the *Oglebay* from Belloy in 1856, and in the following years spent most of his time on Grand Traverse waters, carrying cargo and passengers. On one memorable occasion he took Civil War General Phil Sheridan fishing on Grand Traverse Bay. He liked the General so much that he took him home for dinner. (Sheridan commanded a U. S. government boat investigating smuggling activity on international waters.)

Captain Joe finally retired from sailing and beached the *Oglebay* on the shore in front of his home on the bay. She was getting too old for active service, but he wanted her nearby—they had spent so many years together.

People would see him walking the beaches, gazing nostalgically out over the water. He had a wave and a smile for everyone he met—and some such remark as "Pitty big sea on Gwand Tawbas Bay."

He died at his home on the bay at 77, a seafaring man to the end.

WATER LEVELS IN THE GREAT LAKES

Frequent Question: When will the water level in Lake Michigan start rising again?

Answer: It's a safe bet that the water level will rise sooner or later—if only because water has always done so since the U. S. and Canada started taking regular measurements as long ago as 1865. But there are no guarantees. And nobody knows when.

The present water level in Lake Michigan is down about 4 1/2 feet from its previous high in 1986, and it's still falling. It has about eight or ten inches to go before it matches the record low in 1964.

Unlike the ocean tides, which you can almost set your clock by—they're so regular—long term fluctuations in the Great Lakes water levels are unpredictable. That's because they're mostly controlled by the weather—and we all know how unpredictable that is. (There's a consensus among airline pilots that Michigan has the most unpredictable weather of any place in the nation.) If we get two or three years of cool and wet weather in a row, the lake levels will slowly rise. Conversely, two or three warm and dry years will cause them to fall. It's almost as simple as that.

Other factors enter the equation—evaporation, human and industrial consumption (it's estimated that the average American family uses 100 gallons per person per day) and the amount of outflow from the lakes. But they are dwarfed by the main factor, precipitation.

What about cycles? Doesn't the rise and fall of water in the Great Lakes go in cycles? A local hydrologist says, smiling, "The answer is yes and no. Many hydrologists are skeptical about cycles. They say that the so-called cycles are too erratic. Cycles seem to imply a certain amount of regularity, and there's not much regularity. Without some regularity, there's no predictability. And without some predictability what good are they? Maybe we should call them virtual cycles."

For example, the Great Lakes system experienced extremely low levels in the 1920s, mid-1930s, mid-1960s, and again in the early years of the new century. Extremely high water levels were experienced in the 1870s, early 1950s, mid-1980s, and mid-1990s. Not much regularity there.

In the 1960s, some people were working themselves into a lather about the extremely low levels in Lake Michigan—especially boating people, marinas, and boat manufacturers. They complained that the low water levels were killing them, and they blamed Chicago for taking too much water for its Sanitary and Ship Canal. They circulated petitions and threatened class-action lawsuits. As a result, in 1967 the U. S. Supreme Court limited the diversion to 3,200 cfs (cubic feet per second) averaged over five years.

Not that it mattered. Experts say that Chicago could divert twice as much water without lowering Lake Michigan levels more than an inch or two.

The Great Lakes are among the great wonders of the world. Everything about them is gargantuan. They hold an estimated six quadrillion gallons of water, the largest supply of fresh water on earth. They cover more than 94,000 square miles and drain more than twice as much land. They have nearly 5,800 miles of shoreline. The Great Lakes-St. Lawrence River drainage basin includes part or all of eight U. S. states and two Canadian provinces. Its value is beyond estimation.

A possible long-term threat to the Lakes is global warming and the phenomenon known as the "greenhouse effect." Although debatable, most predictions indicate that global warming would cause prolonged declines in average lake levels into the future. Another potential threat is the growing number of shortages of fresh water in this country and around the world, increasing the pressure to tap the Great Lakes as an alternative supply. So far, authorities have stoutly resisted all such overtures. They say "Don't mess around with Mother Nature."

ONE GOOD TURN DESERVES ANOTHER

In 1909, Charles, Albert, and Arthur Kratochvil organized the Kratochvil Family Band. They got their musical talent from their father, Wencil, who had played French Horn in Traverse City's first band. The fourth member of the four-piece orchestra was James Lyman, whose mother was a Kratochvil. The band played for years at many places around the area, including the Silver Lake Inn.

In 1977, at the age of 90, Charles Kratochvil wrote about something that happened one night in the fall of 1920, when the boys were driving home after an engagement at the Duck Lake Inn. The following is his story, in his own words:

"We were driving home from the Inn in a two-seat buggy with a pair of horses. Art was driving. The road was loose sand through deep timber and big pine stumps. It was pitch dark at three o'clock in the morning.

Suddenly there was a loud crash. The horses stopped dead, and we jumped to the ground. We discovered that one of the wheels had struck a pine stump and was smashed. Being the youngest, I was chosen to go for help. I measured the hub of the wheel and started down the sandy road in my low-cut oxfords, which soon filled with sand. After I had gone a little over a mile I saw a light through the trees. I didn't lose much time getting to it. I rapped on the door and pretty soon a very old man with long whiskers opened it, holding a small lantern. I told him my name and about our misfortune and said I needed a sound buggy wheel.

'Kratochvil is a name I have remembered for a long time,' he said. 'I am going to tell you something that happened a long time ago, probably before you were born. My name is Mason. I own this little gristmill here. One day, many years ago, my wife and I decided to make a trip to Traverse City with the oxen and horses to pick up some supplies for the mill. We got to Traverse City a little after noon, picked up the supplies we needed, and started back about five.

After an hour or so it started to rain. It came down hard. We turned in at a driveway that led past a big log house to a barn. A man came from the house and told us to pull into a big open shed by the barn. By this time the rain was coming down in sheets, and a terrible wind was blowing.

The man said he was Wencil Kratochvil. He took us into the house. He had a big family, some large and some small. Mrs. Kratochvil seemed like a very jolly person and she got us a nice supper. They couldn't do enough for us. After supper we went to look at the weather and it was still raining hard and the Kratochvils insisted we stay the night. Mrs. Kratochvil said, 'We don't have extra beds, but we have lots of extra quilts and blankets. There's lots of room in the guest room, and if you can make yourselves some kind of bed on the floor, we will all be just fine.'

Next morning they gave us breakfast and we thanked them and started on our way. Mr. Kratochvil had given the oxen a big feed of hay so they were all ready to go. I wanted to pay him real good for his trouble and good care he had given us, but he said 'You can't pay me one red cent. I may get into the same fix near your home some day.'

Mr. Mason told me this on our way out to the barn. The first thing I saw there were three good-looking buggy wheels hanging on the wall. I measured one of them, and it was a perfect fit. He took it down from the wall and said, 'It's yours.' I told him I would pay for the wheel now and that I would drop it off as soon as I got a new one in town, and he could keep the money.

He said, 'You will never pay me a red cent for this wheel, here or any place else. You have made me a very happy man tonight. I never forgot your father for what he done for us that night, and I'm sorry I never got to see him again.'

We brought the wheel back two weeks later as I said we would. He met the other boys and we had a long talk and left him a little present. But we never saw him again. We got our first car next year and stopped to see him, but he wasn't home. He passed away soon after that."

BIG FISH

In June of 1934, a huge sturgeon got tangled up in a pond net belonging to Charles Passmore on East Bay. It was a monster, one for the record books. It was six feet six inches long, and it weighed about 150 pounds. It had a girth of three feet.

The fish was in bad shape after floundering around in the net for what must have been several days. Its plight was reported to conservation officers Mark Craw and Frank Hoard. They hastened to the rescue—along with police chief John Blacken; Stanley

Rae, former manager of the Napoleon Auto Company; and Louis Zimmerman, prominent farmer and livestock dealer. The net was located about two miles north of Traverse City near the shore of Old Mission Peninsula.

The five men herded the big fish into a nine-foot gunney sack and towed it to shore. Then then loaded it into a rowboat filled with water and mounted it on an auto trailer, and carried it to the Cass Street fountain. On the way, two of the men in rubber boots rode in the boat to keep the fish from harm.

After lodging it in the fountain pool, Mark Craw told the others that someone had to keep close watch to make sure that the fish didn't turn over on its back and drown. Mark was knowledgeable about things like that.

The big fish seemed to take readily enough to its new, though cramped, environment, and after a few days it appeared to have recovered its strength. During that time, half of Traverse City and the surrounding country came downtown to get a look at it. Finally, Craw and the others returned it to its natural environment in the waters of East Grand Traverse Bay. Mark was a legendary game warden and conservation officer. Born in Antrim County in 1866, he came to Traverse City with his parents. As a young man he was one of the area's outstanding athletes, excelling in running, jumping, and swimming.

He also was the canniest game-law violator of his time, delighting in outwitting the game wardens. Later, he became one of them himself, and his prowess in catching violators red-handed was second to none.

After all, as Mark said, it takes one to catch one, and he knew all the tricks. He spent 45 years with Michigan's Conservation Department as game warden and conservation officer. He died in Traverse City on July 6, 1962, at the age of 96.

The old cobblestone fountain stood in the middle of North Cass Street just north of Cass and Front Streets. It was built in 1924, and a "comfort station" was added a little later, just north of it.

In 1924, automobiles were relatively few on Traverse City streets. As their number grew, however, the fountain and the comfort station came to be regarded as a traffic hazard, and they were removed in 1954.

GOOD NEIGHBORS

The Hohnke farm was almost surrounded by an old Indian camp. The camp had been there as long as anyone could remember. The Hohnkes came from Poland in 1875.

A brook ran through the Hohnke farm. It was fed by a hillside spring. The Indians and the Hohnkes and all the farm animals got water from the spring. It was good cold water, tasting faintly of iron.

The Hohnkes and the Indians were good friends. They got along very well together. Grandma Hohnke said they were fine people, generous and kind. They loved salt pork and fresh baked bread. The Indians raised corn and squash in the village garden. They hunted in the winter.

William Jake was the chief of the tribe. He was a squat, swarthy man. He and his wife Sophia had two children, Eddie and Annie. Sophia's mother lived with them. The Hohnke kids and the Indian kids played together. Sometimes some of the Indians would stay all night at the Hohnke house.

One night in August, Grandma's husband discovered that his horse was gone from the barn. He looked for it but the horse was nowhere around. The next morning though, it was back in the barn. It was all lathered up as if it had been ridden all night. The same thing happened the next night and the next. Grandpa Hohnke knew that one of the young Indians was taking the horse out at night. He was pretty sure he knew which one.

He went to his friend William Jake and told him about it. The Chief said not to worry, it wouldn't happen again. Grandpa figured that the Chief sent him away.

The Chief gave Grandpa a trumpet made of a cattle horn. He told Grandpa to blow a blast on it whenever he needed help—mostly for rounding up cattle. Whenever he summoned help on the horn, the Indians came running. They were good people, Grandpa said. You couldn't ask for better neighbors.

One time Grandma Hohnke had a sore throat. William Jake happened by and she told him about it. He went out in the woods and got some Indian medicine and made herbal syrup. The sore throat went away overnight Grandpa said. She never knew what was in the syrup but it worked fine.

Then came the bad year when almost all of the Indians took sick. It was an epidemic of small pox. The pox spread through the tribe so fast that nothing could be done to stop it. And the Indians died so fast that the others couldn't keep up with burying them. Some crawled away in the woods to die. The Hohnkes did all they could, but there was little they could do. Most of the Indians died. Only a few of the hardiest survived. They scattered to Peshawbestown and Northport and Cross Village—all, that is, but Chief Jake and his family. They lived on in their log house on the campground.

In August of 1920, Hohnke built a house in the village of Leland and he and Grandma went there to live, leaving the farm to their oldest son, William. In 1922 Chief Jake sold his twenty acres to William Hohnke and moved his family to Cross Village.

LAST MAN'S CLUB

In 1919, the Great War to end all wars had barely ended. Adolph Hitler was still unknown, and nobody yet had begun to worry about World War II.

A group of World War I veterans got together and organized American Legion Post No. 35. Charles Sleder was the first commander.

They called it the Bowen-Holliday Post in honor of two local young men who had died in the fighting overseas: 1st Lt. Harry Holliday, commander of an infantry machine gun unit; and Laurence Bowen, a fighter pilot in the British Royal Air Force.

By 1939, 17 men had served as post commander. They were Dr. Dale Gleason, Walter "Pete" Tuttle, Fred Curtis, Ben Koenig, Clarence Anderson, Herman Walters, Albert Peck, Moses Champney, Ray McGarry, Harry Hibbard, Fred Seabrook, Burr Lewis, Frank Wildman, Dr. G. A. Holliday, Charles Sleder, Cecil Sly, and Edward Curtis.

On June 19 of that year they met at the Park Place Hotel for a banquet and formed the "Last Man Club."

Membership was limited to past commanders, and the club roster would be closed with the death of any one of the original members. Until that time, each post commander would be admitted to the club membership upon the close of his term of office.

It was decided to meet for a banquet every year on June 19, the date the Post received its charter. They would continue to meet every year until only two members were left. Those two men would drink a toast to their departed comrades at the final meeting of the club.

For that purpose Moses Champney donated a bottle of Mumms Champagne that he had brought from France after the war. Until that final day, it reposed in a specially built wooden chest lined with satin by Pete Tuttle, whose business was upholstering. With gallows humor they called it "the coffin."

Membership in the club was closed in 1940 with the death of Fred Seabrook. By that time two other members had been added: Wilbur "Speed" Watson and David Wallstead, making a total of 19. One of the members, Moses Champney, had been mayor of Traverse City in 1935 and 1936. Two others, Ben Koenig and Wilbur Watson, served as mayor in 1945 and 1950 respectively.

By 1952 only 10 men were left, and in 1960 more than half were gone. But the banquet table was still set for 19—at the place of each departed member, a la Omar Khayyam, they "turned down an empty glass." By the 1960s there were so many empty chairs that the mood, though still resolutely cheerful, was tinged with a bit of melancholy.

In 1961, to liven things up a bit, the sons of the living members (and of the recently deceased Fred Seabrook) were secretly rounded up—some of them from faraway places—and introduced as a surprise.

The meeting was held as usual in the Queen's Room at the Park Place Hotel, but part of the room was partitioned off by a screen. Then, after the members were seated at their own table, the screen was drawn to reveal the sons seated at the other table. It was a dramatic and touching moment.

After the death of Harry Hibbard and Wilbur Watson in 1974, only two surviving members, Pete Tuttle and Dr. Dale Gleason, were left.

Accordingly, on the 19th of June that year the two of them held the final meeting of the Last Man Club. They uncorked Moses Champney's bottle of champagne (it didn't pop), and drank a final toast to their departed friends. Then they passed the bottle around the table so that family members, who had joined them for the last ceremony, could have a sip.

The wine itself was disappointing. Unlike whiskey and brandy, wine doesn't improve beyond a certain age.

Pete Tuttle said, "Oh, it tasted like champagne, but the fizz was gone."

His daughter-in-law was even less enthusiastic. She said it tasted like vinegar. (Which wasn't surprising for wine that had lain around in a "coffin" all those years.)

Dr. Gleason died in 1976. He was followed by Walter "Pete" Tuttle on September 26, 1985. And that was the end of the "Last Man Club."

A WOMAN'S WORK IS NEVER DONE

Today's women find it hard to understand how pioneer women with all the work they had to do—washing, ironing, mending, sewing, cooking, baking, churning, and gardening—ever found time to get some sleep. Yet they never considered themselves drudges. Like the men, they took the work for granted, and they managed to socialize with the neighbors and have a bit of fun too, once in a while.

On April 19, 1862, strong, attractive Lavinia Lindley married William Mebert, a cultured German immigrant, and settled in a log house south of Suttons Bay on the newly opened State Road. Lavinia kept a diary during the years 1864 and 1865. Written in a plain and simple but articulate style, it paints a vivid picture of life on the western frontier. The following are excerpts from the diary:

(May 1, 1864) William and I went down to Mr. Cunningham and bought a bushel of potatoes.

(May 15) William and I started for Suttons Bay to attend church. Everything went very pleasantly and we came home again in good spirits. Little Henry stayed with his uncle and was a good boy. We saw five deer tracks.

(May 23) Little Henry's birthday, one year old.

(May 27) James Lee came and invited William to the raising and myself to spend the day with Miss and Mrs. Lee.

(June 14) Mr. Cumberworth came and invited William and self to a quilting party at his home.

(July 7) Rev. George N. Smith called

(July 9) Baked and sewed some on my bloomers.

(July 10) Finished my bloomers.

(July 22) Put ruffles on my dress. Commenced Henry's petticoat and William's overalls. Made Henry a pair of stockings.

(July 30) Dressed myself and baby and we started for the Lees. William married Miss Mary Weigand to John Lee. We stayed until one or two o'clock.

(August 1) Little Henry taken sick this morning about 1 o'clock, growing worse all day. In the evening he had a very bad fit, so William and I took him down to father's.

(August 2) Little Henry is much better . . . Since I wrote the above my little son has come very near to dying, but thank God, he is getting better now. Oh, how thankful I am!

(Feb. 5, 1865) Mrs. W. Steele called. Commenced to wash and Mrs. Sutton came. I put my washing away and visited. Commenced washing again and Miss Rose Miller Gonyan and two or three others came and so of course I had to put my washing away and get dinner for them. Asenath came. After dinner I finished washing. Finished embroidering a pair of drawers for Little Henry and read.

(Feb. 12) William and I all alone with our baby. Read and enjoyed ourselves capitally.

(Sept. 1) Mr. Stimel's and Groesser's little girls here.

(Sept. 4) James commenced cutting his house logs today.

(Sept. 5) James and Asenath moved up this morning. Worked hard putting things to rights. William is to marry a couple this evening, Mr. Curry and Miss Ada Palmer.

(Sept. 9) Ann came, brought Mother's sauce plates for me to use, and I being very busy, had no time to take care of them. So Little Henry played with them unbeknownst to me and broke two of them. In the evening I had company come, and 20 or 30 had supper, then danced until twelve o'clock. All seemed to enjoy themselves. Well, I'm sure I did.

HOW MANY MILES TO WALK?

B ack in the days before tractors replaced horses, how many miles did a farmer have to walk to raise 10 acres of corn?

Jerome Black of Traverse City, who was born on a farm near Buckley in the early 1920s, has done the calculations. At the age of eight he was already driving a team of plough horses all by himself. At the age of 14, however, he decided he didn't want to be a farmer.

Walking Distances
(A typical 10-acre field is 40 rods square.)

Ploughing:

With a single plow drawn by two horses, the furrow is about 14 inches wide. The first round would be exactly 1/2 mile. Each subsequent round would be 52 inches wide. Total walking distance— 71 miles.

Dragging:

In preparing the ground for planting the farmer would drag the area 3 times with a 5-foot drag and one horse. Total walking distance—50 miles.
Planting:

Marking out the hills to be planted, two men holding a 16-foot pole with small chains attached at the proper intervals would walk back and forth in both directions over the ground to be planted. Each hill of corn would be planted where the lines intersected. Total walking distance—21 miles.

Planting:
A hand-operated corn-planter was used to drop the kernels on the marked spot. The farmer would step on the spot to cover and pack the dirt over the planted kernels. Total distance—31 miles.

Cultivating:
With a single cultivator drawn by one horse, the farmer would hold the cultivator close to the row of corn on one side and back on the other side. The corn usually would be cultivated 3 times during the growing season. For the last time, the cultivator would be set to go in the center of the rows instead of close to the row. Total walking distance—154 miles.

Harvesting:
A sawhorse with a handle through it would be placed at the center of eight square hills of corn. With a sickle in hand the farmer would cut each hill and place it at the sawhorse so as to form a shock. After all stalks in the quarter had been cut and stacked, the farmer would bind the shocks with binder twine and go on to the next eight hills. Total walking distance—64 miles.
Total Distance: 391 miles.

O
PIONEERS!

THE OPEN SPACE

What's the Open Space?" an unidentified man who called the other day wanted to know.

"It's the open space on the bay at the end of Union Street by the zoo."

"Yeah, but what do they call it?"

"They call it the Open Space."

"Who's on third?" the man said cheerfully, and hung up.

It all began when the old Hannah, Lay Lumber Company building and the J. C. Morgan canning plant were torn down in 1950 to make way for the Grandview Parkway. The big Hannah, Lay docks also were dismantled. (Legend has it that one of the demolition workers on the Hannah, Lay building was attacked by a horde of rats in that creepy, crawly place and ran off down the street in a panic.)

The city cleaned up the site, planted grass, flowers, and shrubs, and turned it into a lovely waterfront park. For lack of a more specific name, people started calling it "the open space", and somehow it stuck. It wasn't until about ten years ago that a few people suggested that a more imaginative name should be selected. Among the suggestions were Morgan Park and, perhaps in jest, Cannery Row.

But a random poll, by no means scientific, indicated that many more people were happy with "Open Space" and wanted to keep it so. They were used to it, they liked the sound of it, and—however clunky it might seem to some people—they saw no reason to change it.

THE SAGA OF CAPTAIN DAN SEAVEY

The Captain never carried a weapon, except his fists. Yet over the course of a long and boisterous life he was accused of almost every crime in the book—including piracy, smuggling, poaching, stealing, pillaging, hijacking and bootlegging, arson, manslaughter and even murder—and was never convicted of any one of them. The problem was, with such a flamboyant and legendary character as Dan Seavey, it was difficult to separate fact from fiction.

He was born in Portland, Maine, in 1868, left home at the age of twelve or thirteen and went to sea, sailing on tramp steamers. Later, when he came of age, he did a hitch in the U. S. Navy. But Dan never liked taking orders. Following Horace Greeley's advice to young men, he headed west to Wisconsin and Minnesota.

First he got a job with the Department of Indian Affairs. Later he opened a fish market and two saloons in Milwaukee, and even tried his hand at farming. In 1898 he sold all his possessions, joined the Gold Rush to the Yukon, and like most amateur prospectors, came home empty-handed. But his heart was always in open waters and by some manner or means he acquired a little two-masted schooner called *Wanderer*, and began hauling freight (at least some of it probably stolen) to all Lake Michigan ports.

In addition to sailing, Dan loved drinking, fighting, and youngsters. One classic story originated in Escanaba, where Dan made his home for several years. Children were always welcome aboard when *Wanderer* was in port. They were fascinated by Dan's tales of life at sea. One of them, the son of a well-to-do Escanaba businessman, had been forbidden by his father to go aboard because of Dan's reputation as a drunken brawler. But the lad couldn't resist temptation and one day his father caught him on deck and ordered him to come down at once. When he obeyed, his father turned him over one knee and gave him a sound spanking. Seavey caught sight of the spectacle and hastened down the gang plank. He seized the man, turned him over his knee, and gave him a sound spanking.

"Don't ever lay a hand on one of my shipmates!" he roared.

Seavey never picked a fight, but he never turned one down, either. At a saloon in Naubinway he was provoked into a fight by a notorious thief and smuggler of whiskey to the Indians. Both went at it, tooth and nail, no holds barred, for the better part of an hour, pausing only for a drink now and then. The two men were pretty evenly matched, but Dan finally knocked his opponent down and out; and to keep him down, Dan upended a piano on his neck. Unfortunately, when Dan removed the piano, the man didn't stir, and died the next day.

WHERE DID FATHER MARQUETTE DIE?

On May 18, 1675, Jesuit priest Jacques Marquette, who with explorer Louis Joliet "discovered" the Mississippi River (never mind that the American Indians had discovered it thousands of years earlier), died and was buried by his two French boatmen and companions on the bank of a river somewhere along the east coast of Lake Michigan.

Two years later his remains were disinterred and brought to his mission at St. Ignace by a group of Kiskakon Ottawa Indians, who loved the gentle young priest and were devoted members of his flock.

The exact site of Marquette's death has long been a matter of conjecture and dispute. The State of Michigan has awarded historical markers to both Ludington and Frankfort, seeming to imply that the good priest died at both places, which is not only unlikely but obviously impossible.

Now comes Robert P. Adams, whose book *The Thirteenth River*, makes a powerful argument for a third contender. He claims that Pere Marquette died at neither Frankfort nor Ludington, but at Manistee, and he has marshaled a compelling body of scientific evidence to prove it.

In 1978, Adams, a lifelong resident of Manistee, embarked on a research project that would last nearly 20 years. Its primary purpose was to try to resolve the dispute between Frankfort and Ludington. He approached the problem from the perspective of an engineer and mathematician; he was after cold facts, not hearsay. It was only much later, when the scientific evidence began to show a consistent pattern, that he came to the surprising conclusion that the actual site of Marquette's death was Manistee.

Adams spent years studying all the historical documents that deal with Marquette's life and death. Among the most important of these is the story by Jesuit missionary Claude Dablon in the *Jesuit Relations* in 1677. Dablon got his information about the priest's death and a description of the site from Marquette's two companions, boatmen Pierre Porteret and Jacques Largilliers.

Another primary document is a journal kept by explorer-priest Pierre F. X. Charlevoix on an exploratory trip down the east coast of Lake Michigan in 1721. Charlevoix was interested in finding the actual site where Marquette died (which had become uncertain in the 45 years since his death), and he carefully checked and recorded the latitude and the geographical features of Michigan river mouths from the Platte River to the Big Manistee.

Other documents of equal importance are the so-called Charlevoix Map of 1744 (based on his Journal) and the Franquelin Map of 1684 (based on Ferdinand LaSalle's Expeditions of 1679-80-81-82). The Charlevoix map shows twelve rivers, the Franquelin map only eight.

Adams capped his research project by following in Charlevoix's tracks. He bought a 28-foot voyageur canoe and recruited a crew of paddlers from among his Manistee friends. Over a period of five years, usually in the month of August, he examined all the river-ends where Charlevoix had been, comparing their latitudes and geographical features with the entries in Charlevoix's Journal.

Adams was impressed by Charlevoix's accuracy. With only slight variances, Charlevoix's latitude numbers tally closely with his own. Adams attributes the differences to the medieval instrument Charlevoix used, the astrolabe, which is much harder to read than the more modern quadrant. Adams is proficient in the use of both instruments.

But one reading puzzled him. Charlevoix listed one latitude where no river exists today. Upon further research Adams found that it marks the location of Portage Creek, which in Charlevoix's time flowed from Portage Lake to Lake Michigan. Adams also found that the creek was deliberately eradicated on May 7, 1871.

Adams believes that Charlevoix made a curious mistake—he identified Portage Creek (the "thirteenth river") as the site of Marquette's death.

"He came close," Adams says, "but no cigar. He missed it by only nine miles. Portage Creek is nine miles north of the Manistee River."

But Portage Creek was no river. And Charlevoix knew that. So why the error?

Nevertheless, Adams buttresses his claim for Manistee with an impressive mass of physical and scientific evidence.

"Manistee is the only site that fits all the numbers and the geography," he says. "In any case, Frankfort and Ludington don't."

Will the State of Michigan award Manistee a third historical Marquette marker?

Don't hold your breath.

THE MAN WHO CAPTURED PERRY HANNAH

In 1854, a group of Bohemian emigrants left their native land and sailed for America from Bremerhaven, Germany, in the *Herzogin* a two-masted German schooner not much bigger than Columbus's Pinto. They landed at New York after a stormy voyage of 52 days, then went on to Chicago by train, arriving on Christmas Day. Finally it dawned on them that they were on the wrong continent.

Somehow they had mistakenly believed that they were headed for Brazil, which they thought was part of the United States—a kind of "Garden of Eden" where the living was easy and all kinds of fruit and nuts grew on trees, free for the picking. They didn't like Chicago. Chicago was built on a swamp and there were mud-puddles with green scum everywhere. Shortly after their arrival there, they chose three men to scout the Grand Traverse region, where, they had been told, good land was available for homesteading. They were Gotleib Greilick, Joseph Shalda, and Frank Kratochvil. They landed at Good Harbor in Leelanau County in the spring of 1885.

Shalda liked the Good Harbor area and stayed there. Greilick and Kratochvil traveled overland to the foot of Grand Traverse Bay, where Greilick chose to make his home in the place—Greilickville—that still bears his name. Kratochvil and his son Wencil went on to Traverse City, where they found work at the Hannah, Lay & Company sawmill. All three men of the advance party soon brought their families up from Chicago. They arrived on Hannah Company's *Telegraph* that same year.

148

The Kratochvil family of nine spent their first night under a tree, and were almost eaten alive by mosquitoes. Finally they persuaded the company foreman, Cuyler Germaine, to let them occupy a shack on the Hannah dock. At night they could see the stars through big holes in the roof, but Frank and Wencil fixed that by covering them with bark.

Wencil's job was to help load lumber on lake schooners. Frank was hired as watchman. Both earned eight dollars a month plus room and board. Frank took his job very seriously, and there is a story handed down in the family that bears retelling.

One night Frank collared a man wandering about the lumberyard. Frank marched the intruder to the watchman's shack, sat him down by the stove, and held him captive. In vain the man protested that he was Perry Hannah, who owned the place. But Frank, who spoke no English, was adamant, and finally Perry settled down to make the best of it.

When the morning came the day crew found Perry Hannah still under guard in the watchman's shack, and they berated Frank for his treatment of the boss man.

But Hannah—whose habit it was to prowl around the mill and the lumberyard at night, looking for possible trouble—calmed them down.

"Leave this man alone," he said. "He was only doing his job. That's what I pay him for."

WHO WAS R. FLOYD CLINCH?

Most Traverse City people know that Clinch Park was named after R. Floyd Clinch, but only a few know much about him. Local historians have somehow overlooked this man. Yet in 1930 he was honored by the Chamber of Commerce as Traverse City's outstanding citizen of the year, and he became the first winner of the Chamber's Distinguished Service Award.

Clinch was born in Georgia in 1875, the son of Col. Duncan L. Clinch of the Confederate Army and the grandson of Gen. Duncan L. Clinch, who served in the War of 1812. Floyd came to Chicago in 1883 and embarked on a highly successful career in business and finance. He helped organize the became president of Crerar-Clinch Coal Company, operating 16 mines in Ohio and Illinois, and of the Auditorium Hotel Company. He was an officer and director of many large corporations, including the Chicago Rapid Transit company (elevated lines), Chicago & North Western Railroad, Central Illinois Trust Company, and the Michigan Transit Company boat line. Among his closest business and social friends were U. S. Vice President Charles G. Dawes and the renowned public utilities tycoon Samuel Insull, whose empire collapsed in 1934 amid charges of embezzlement, of which he was later cleared. Dawes and Insull were Clinch's guests here in Traverse City when he entertained his fellow directors of the Illinois Trust Company in August of 1928.

Clinch's involvement in Traverse City affairs was almost accidental. Soon after he came to Chicago, he married Katherine Lay, the daughter of Albert Tracy Lay, vice-president of Hannah, Lay & Company. Along with Perry Hannah and James Morgan, Lay was one of the original founders of the company. Hannah was in charge of company interests in Traverse City, and Lay looked after the business in Chicago; Morgan was a silent partner, as was his brother William, who later was admitted to the partnership.

Perry Hannah died in 1904, and his son Julius, who had been groomed to take over the company, died the following year. Leadership of the company thus fell on Tracy Lay's shoulders. He, however, declined the responsibility because of advanced age and asked his son-in-law R. Floyd Clinch to become active head of the corporation.

Clinch wanted to become more than just a representative of his father-in-law in Traverse City; so in his own right he bought the Morgan interests, and assumed the title of vice president until the death of Tracy Lay in 1918, when he became president.

From that time on, Clinch spent nearly half his time in Traverse City. Here he had charge of three Hannah, Lay corporations: Traverse City State Bank, Boardman River Light & Electric Power Company, and Hannah, Lay Mercantile Company. In 1930 he built the new Park Place Hotel—the city's tallest and most familiar landmark—replacing the historic old wooden structure built in 1873 by Henry D.

Campbell; and he had plans to erect a new two-story brick annex in the style of the nine-story hotel. He was also among the leaders in the development of plans for the waterfront park that bears his name. And he was a major benefactor in many civic and industrial projects, including the National Music Camp at Interlochen.

Clinch died of a heart attack in his office in the Rookery Building in Chicago at noon on November 7, 1930. His son, Duncan L. Clinch, followed his father's example as a civic and business leader in Traverse City: the Clinch Park Marina was named after him.

Incidentally, despite widespread popular belief, R. Floyd Clinch did not donate the land for Clinch Park. The distinction of providing land for the park belongs to another prominent Traverse City man, Con Foster.

PETER DOUGHERTY AND OLD MISSION

In May 1839, a Mackinaw boat with four men and three passengers rounded a point that juts out from what is now known as Old Mission Peninsula and forms a small cove now called Old Mission Harbor. The passengers were Reverend Peter Dougherty and Reverend Peter Fleming, missionaries of the Presbyterian Board, and Peter Greensky, their Indian interpreter. They had spent the previous winter at Mackinac Island and now had come to Traverse Bay country to establish a mission among the Indians.

At the Indian village, which consisted of a few bark-covered teepees, they were met by a single Indian. He told them that the tribe was camped across the bay at the mouth of the river where Elk Rapids is today. He sent them a message by smoke signal and within a short time a canoe loaded with Indian men arrived at the cove. They asked the strangers who they were and what they wanted.

Next day, a chief with several other men landed at the cove. The missionaries explained that they had been sent by Indian Agent Henry Schoolcraft and the great white chief in Washington to establish a school for the Indian children and educate them in the white man's ways and the Christian religion. (Never mind that the

Indians probably preferred their own ways and their own religion but were too polite to say so.) The emissaries replied that they would take the message to their head chief, Aishquagwonaba, and that he would probably pay them a visit before long.

Several days later, Aishquagwonaba and the other chiefs gathered together for a council meeting, after which the missionaries were informed that the local Indians had decided to unite the bands and locate near the river on the east side of bay. If the missionaries were willing, they would show them where the new villages would be located, and they could choose a good central site for their dwelling and school. The missionaries, with some reluctance, were willing.

Around the 20th of May, the white men in their Mackinaw boat together with a fleet of Indian canoes, landed at the mouth of Elk River. The Indians planned to divide their settlement into two villages. The missionaries chose a location about a quarter mile south of the river. With the help of Peter Greensky, they began cutting logs for their lodging and school.

In spite of the heat and sand flies, work on the house and school progressed at a good pace, but then fate dealt a heavy blow to one of the missionaries. A messenger from Mackinac Island brought Peter Fleming the sad news that his wife had died there. Fleming departed immediately in the same boat that had brought him here, never to return.

Around the 20th of June, Chief Aghosa of the Mission Harbor band approached Peter Dougherty and said that his people weren't willing to move to the east side of the bay. He offered to transport him and his baggage across to Mission Harbor and to build him a house he could live in. Dougherty needed no persuasion—he was convinced that the harbor site was the better of the two. After a day or two, leaving what wasn't needed for immediate use and loading the other baggage in Indian canoes, Dougherty and Greensky were ferried across the water to their new home.

In their absence, Henry Schoolcraft in a small sailing vessel arrived at the Mission cove and dropped off an Indian blacksmith, Isaac George; and in the fall, another government employee, Indian farmer John Johnston, arrived at the settlement. In 1841, Henry

Bradley became an additional teacher, and David McGulpin, assistant farmer.

That same month, the tiny settlement had a pleasant surprise. Peter and Maria Dougherty and their baby daughter Henrietta arrived in a small schooner from Mackinac, where both parents had waited until after the baby was born.

In the fall of 1842, there were five log buildings, a schoolhouse and dwellings and in 1843, a Mission church of hewn cedar timbers.

By 1850, the tiny settlement had grown to a considerable size. It had become famous as a stopping place for some of the earliest Traverse City pioneers, including Stephen Wait and Lewis Miller.

WHO WAS ORSON PECK?

Orson Peck was the guy who produced the famous postcard of a streetcar on Front Street. It fooled a lot of people of later generations into believing that it was accurate. So did another well-known postcard showing the new Pere Marquette Railroad station at the corner of Lake and Union Streets.

Of course, no streetcar ever made an appearance on Front Street, and no new PM Railroad station was ever built at Union and Lake streets. Both photos are composites: depot and streetcar were dubbed in. But Peck wasn't trying to fool anybody. Both projects had been planned for many years around the turn of the century. Peck was just anticipating a reality that never came about.

Well, maybe it isn't quite that simple. Peck had a lively imagination and a great sense of humor. He was always fooling around with reality. He delighted in putting people and things into his photos. He wasn't satisfied, for example, with just a beautiful photograph of a sunset on Grand Traverse Bay; he'd dub in a sailboat or two. One local historian claims he never saw a Peck postcard that hadn't been enhanced in some way. Peck produced hundreds of them. All are collectors' items today.

Peck was a completely self-taught photographer. He made a good living producing postcards of the Grand Traverse region and elsewhere. One particular card—of birch trees on Silver Lake—sold nearly half a million copies.

Peck worked with a large view-camera on a wooden tripod. Until film became available he used glass-plate negatives. Before 1914 he sent his color postcards—which he himself colored by hand— to Germany for printing.

"He was a perfectionist," said Norma Cotter, who worked for Peck in the 1930s. "He would spend hours, sometimes even days, getting the picture he wanted. He was a stickler for quality. The only time he ever scolded me was one day when I made some mistakes while trying to turn out the cards too fast.

"'Remember,' he told me, 'in this shop we turn out quality, not quantity.'"

Orson W. Peck (the W did not stand for anything) was born in Saginaw on August 31, 1875, and came to Traverse City with his parents at the age of 13. His father was a conductor on the Grand Rapids & Indiana Railroad. Orson got little more than an eighth grade education—most days he played hookey. He told Cotter that he had decided, early on, that he wasn't going to work on the railroad, and that he wasn't going to do any manual labor.

His intense concentration on photography—to the exclusion of almost everything else—gave him a reputation for eccentricity. He seemed not to care about anything else. After a brief marriage that produced one son and ended in divorce, he lived alone in his house and studio at 807 Washington Street.

Margaret Fiebing, who worked for him one summer, running his small, hand-operated printing press, recalls him as a man of strange ways—particularly in regard to food.

"He wouldn't take time to prepare a hot meal," she said. "For supper he might open a can of beans and eat them cold. He just couldn't be bothered with cooking. He'd buy a case of canned peaches and maybe for a week he'd eat nothing but peaches and crackers. But then he'd get so sick of peaches he could't bear to look at them ever again."

Peck had little time for socializing or recreation. He had no religious affiliation and claimed to be an atheist or at least an agnostic. Yet he loved his mother dearly (she lived across the street from him) and after she died he regularly put flowers on her grave.

Fiebing said she twitted him about that, asking why he took such pains if he had no belief in any hereafter.

Peck smiled and said it was "…just in case." He died at home on June 15, 1954, at the age of 79.

WHO WAS CON FOSTER?

When Conrad H. Foster first came to town, people didn't quite know what to make of him. What they saw was a tall, thin, mildly profane but nevertheless soft-spoken man with tousled white hair and a gruff manner, wearing steel-rimmed spectacles and a cigar stub in one corner of his mouth. Some called him crusty. But his good friend Mayor James T. Milliken—whom Foster didn't like at first—said he was the kindest, most generous man he'd ever met.

He was also a visionary. He was also a showman.

What made him seem a bit odd was his relentless, single-minded pursuit of money—money not for its own sake or for himself, but for the common good. Actually he cared little about money, except as a means to that end. It kept him busy walking up and down Front Street raising money for his projects from all the merchants and almost every one he met. A friend said that every time he met Con Foster on the street it cost him money. Ultimately, his efforts paid big dividends. Far more than any other individual, Con Foster was the driving force behind the magic transformation of a municipal dumping ground into a beautiful waterfront park called Clinch.

Con Foster moved his family here in 1920 after spending most of his life as an executive for Ringling Brothers Barnum & Bailey Circus and as a trouble-shooter for the Butterfield movie theater chain. It didn't take him long to make his presence known. He attended all meetings of the City Commission and wasn't a bit bashful about offering suggestions and occasional criticism. Although both the commission and the voters turned him down, he never lost his vision of a waterfront park.

One of his first steps was the organization of 52 men who contributed a total of $10,000 in December of 1925 to buy what was known then as the Ott property—former site of the Hannah, Lay sawmill complex. Ultimately, the men deeded the 784 foot long strip of land between the bay and the Boardman River to the city. Again without any help from the city, he raised funds for a native Michigan aquarium in 1930, the first building at Clinch Park.

Foster wasn't daunted by the opposition. "It doesn't matter whether the taxpayers like it or not," Foster once said. "This park will make money for them. Our town makes its living on tourists, and the show we've got here is bringing a hundred thousand extra ones every year."

Foster later won a seat on the City Commission and also served as City Parks Commissioner. Along with city engineer Charles Sawyer, he was able to get funds for other projects from the federal Works Progress Administration, including the Clinch Park breakwater, the city zoo, the miniature Traverse City, and Con Foster Museum.

The museum was built by government workers in the winter of 1934 and opened to the public in the summer of 1935. Foster used his own money traveling all over the Midwest to obtain collections of pioneer and Indian relics for his museum.

Foster loved animals. "I can remember my father showing Clyde Beatty, the famous lion-tamer, around the city zoo," says Helen Keene, Foster's daughter. "All during the tour, Dad had a pet baby skunk in his pocket. When he held out the little critter to Beatty, the lion tamer flinched. He said he'd rather face his big cats than a skunk."

Foster was elected mayor in 1936. By that time he had almost become a legend in his own time. He was a familiar figure on Front Street, greeting people in front of his Michigan Theater. He would be quick to collar anyone who tried to sneak past the ticket window, but kids who didn't have the money usually got in free.

Con Foster, having received all the honors a grateful community could bestow, died in 1940. Mission accomplished.

A MAN NAMED CAMPBELL

History has slighted Henry Campbell: hardly anyone today has ever heard of him. Yet he was unquestionably—after Perry Hannah—the most influential man in Traverse City history. He probably held more public offices and initiated more successful business enterprises than anyone else, including Perry Hannah.

He wasn't much to look at: a stumpy little man, but rock solid, he resembled one of Walt Disney's seven dwarves—especially after he grew long whiskers. He was five feet tall, but nevertheless a human dynamo of energy and ambition, a big man in every other way but physical stature.

Campbell was born in New York state in 1831. He joined his parents in Traverse City in 1852, and like almost every other man in the village at that time worked for Perry Hannah, first in the woods in 1852 and 1853, then as tally man in the sawmill the following summer. He spent the next six years managing the Hannah, Lay company's office and store on Bay Street as bookkeeper, salesman, and cashier. He also served on the first grand jury in the county and opened the first post office in Traverse City. For four years he also served as the county's first treasurer, conducted the first tax sale, and made the first delivery of tax money to the state, directed the building of the road between Traverse City and Acme, served 12 years as probate judge, and built the Campbell Block at 225 East Front Street, for many years home of the Elks Club.

Yet somehow in the midst of all this enterprise and activity Campbell always found time to indulge his greatest love—hunting and fishing. After moving to Traverse City from his farm home, he died—as doubtless he would have wished—with his boots on. He was shoveling snow from his sidewalk the morning of February 4, 1902 at age 71.

BIRNEY J. MORGAN, ENTREPRENEUR

They called him BeeJay—a big congenial, open-hearted man with a round cherubic Irish face and a toothbrush mustache. One of Traverse City's most successful self-made men, he parlayed a livestock business, livery stable, farming, canning, lumbering and banking into a small empire.

Morgan came here with his father (his mother had died) from Camden, Lorain County, Ohio, where he was born in 1846. His first job was at the Gunton House, a hotel at the corner of Front and Wellington Streets. Twelve years later he married the owner's daughter, Carrie M. Gunton, and they had three children, two daughters and a son. In 1869 he established the first livery stable, on State Street, henceforth known as Morgan's Pioneer Livery.

Morgan was the first big importer of farm horses into the Grand Traverse area. Until then, oxen were used almost exclusively on northern Michigan farms. Oxen are much stronger than horses and can pull much heavier loads; but they are much slower and less maneuverable than horses; they can't back up. For years, Morgan bought thousands of horses in Ohio, Indiana, and southern Michigan, and herded them north to Traverse City. It was BeeJay who made oxen obsolete in this area.

Later, he became interested in lumbering. He built a sawmill on South Manitou Island and logged off most of the island's big timber. He also operated a sawmill and shingle mill at Cobb's Junction in the Boardman River Valley.

From the beginning, Morgan was actively engaged in farming, and owned several farms in the Traverse area. In the 1890s he established one of the first commercial orchards on 10 acres in Elmwood Township, on M-72 just west of Grand Traverse Bay. And in 1902, in partnership with Perry Hannah and Dr. D. C. Kneeland, he built the town's first cherry canning factory; it was known as the Traverse City Canning Company. It was located on Hall Street north of Front, where later in the same building, Red Mill Lumber Company did business for many years. At that time, Morgan was one of the principal stockholders in and president of First National Bank, which opened its doors in 1885, the second bank in town. (Traverse City State Bank was the first.)

The list of BeeJay's accomplishments goes on and on. He was active in local politics and somehow managed to find the time to serve two terms as Grand Traverse County Sheriff. Morgan was said to be one of the most generous men in town, and that his purse was always open to worthy causes and needy people.

That was a fitting epitaph for Birney J. Morgan, who died at 61 in his spacious home on State Street on July 24, 1910. A lot of Traverse City people were sorry to see him go.

DOUGHERTY AND NEW MISSION

The Indians at Old Mission were restless. They were restless because by the Treaty of 1850 they were permitted to buy land. Some restrictions were involved: only "civilized" Indians need apply. ("Civilized" meant belonging to no tribe.) In addition, the only available land was on the west side of Grand Traverse Bay but not yet on Old Mission Peninsula.

Among the many services that Peter Dougherty had performed for his Indians was his annual trip to Mackinac Island to collect their annuities and to keep them safe from the hands of unscrupulous traders who sold them cheap whiskey. Dougherty encouraged Chief Aghosa and his band to buy land with their annuities and helped them in the transactions.

With the gradual scattering of his flock, Dougherty decided to move the mission across the bay to what is now the Omena area and in the spring of 1852 he followed Chief Aghosa and his band. The move was made aboard a sloop carrying all the Dougherty household belongings and those of Lewis Miller and is family and George Craker, who was to spend the next 14 years teaching farming to the Indians.

The land that Dougherty bought for his new mission for the Chippewa bordered on a band of Ottawa Indians under Chief Shabwasung. But both had long-standing brotherly ties and spoke the same language. Shabwasung's people had been there for a long time; there were apple trees in their gardens the girth of a man's body.

Dougherty's New Mission focused primarily on the Indian children, many of whose parents had bought land in the Omena area. With lumber and other building material brought over from Old Mission, Dougherty built a two-story schoolhouse and living quarters for some 50 children. It had separate rooms for boys and girls. The girls were taught cooking and sewing, and the boys were taught farming. Both studied reading and writing.

In 1858 Dougherty built a church in the Early American Colonial style. It was dedicated as Grove Hill New Mission Church. Gleaming white and looking as if it had been built just yesterday, it still stands on a little hill overlooking Omena Bay. It was constructed of the finest white pine lumber, brought over from a sawmill in Green Bay, Wisconsin. The carpenters were William Putt, Robert Campbell, and Eusebius Dame.

The church has changed very little in almost 150 years. Originally it had two front doors; they were replaced by windows and a double door cut between them. Church services are still held every Sunday in the summer. In 1975, the church was officially registered as one of Michigan's Historic Sites.

The same bell that summoned the Indians to Sunday services at Old Mission now hangs in the church belfry at Omena; they brought it over to New Mission when they came. Tradition has it that the great bell was cast from large British copper pennies collected by the Indians for their services in the War of 1812 and given as a tribute for their friend Peter Dougherty, who sent them to a foundry for casting.

In his conversations with the Indians, Dougherty often used the word "Omena" which means "Is it so?". As in English, it is more a comment than a question. The Indians were amused by Dougherty's habit and they suggested that the settlement be given that name.

Dougherty and the Indians had a strong bond of friendship. One of the few exceptions was Chief Asabun, who refused to go to church services because Dougherty wouldn't let him smoke his pipe there. (In his diary, Dougherty calls him "Old Snake.") The Indians called Dougherty "Mikoos", meaning "Little Beaver."

He was a good man who had spent a good part of his life helping a disadvantaged people whose way of life for hundreds of years was crumbling before their eyes. (In recent years, the Indians have staged a comeback, improving their economic condition and preserving some of their ancient culture. We wish them well.)

For lack of church funds, New Mission closed down in 1868, and Dougherty moved his family to Somers, Wisconsin. He died there on February 15, 1894.

PERRY HANNAH

Perry Hannah, known even during his lifetime as the "Father of Traverse City" was arguably the closest thing to a great man that the city ever had. He stands out over prominent men not only for what he did, which was prodigious, but also for what he was. A man with a cool eye, someone said of him, recalling the poet Yeats' great lines: "Cast a cold eye/ on life, on death/ Horseman, pass by!"

For more than fifty years Perry Hannah was synonymous with Traverse City. And surprisingly (for men of great wealth and power usually manage to pick up at least a few enemies along the way) he was also Traverse City's most highly respected citizen. Although he was seldom seen in public without his long, double breasted frock-coat, vest, starched white color, top hat and bow-tie, he wasn't above joining his lumberjacks in log rolling contests on the Boardman River on the Fourth of July. A man of dignity, but also with a common touch.

He was born on a farm in Erie County, Pennsylvania on September 22, 1824. At the age of thirteen he joined his father (his mother had died young) and helped him raft logs from Port Huron to Detroit. In 1846 he took a job as a clerk in Jacob Beidler's lumber yard in Chicago. In 1846, with Beidler's help, he formed a partnership with two other young men, Albert Lay and William Morgan, known as Hannah, Lay & Company. Shortly after that, the firm bought the Boardman mill and property on Grand Traverse Bay.

During the first few years Hannah and Tracy Lay took turns in looking after business in Traverse City and Chicago, each spending six months here and six months in Chicago. After 1855 Hannah took permanent charge of the Traverse City end of the business, while Lay remained in Chicago.

Perry Hannah served as president of the village from the time of its incorporation in 1881 until it became a city in 1895; he was the city's first mayor. In 1857 he represented the district in the Michigan Legislature, traveling to Lansing on snowshoes with an Indian guide. He donated the land for all of the early churches and public buildings. He built the first railroad in 1872, the first big general store, the first bank. For fifty years he presided over an empire of lumbering, shipping, milling, banking, merchandising, and real estate. He was a man of intellect and eloquence. Elvin L. Sprague, editor of the *Daily Eagle*, interviewed Hannah in his late years and wrote: "He thinks the hereafter is a mystery which no man knows anything of but feels he has led a respectable life and is ready to meet the uncertainty with courage, taking his chances with the rest of humanity."

Hannah died on August 16, 1904; his funeral was the biggest ever held in Traverse City. The birth and development of the city he loved had been in good hands.

HARRY SUTTON AND SUTTONS BAY

Suttons Bay had three different names in succession: Suttonsburg, Pleasant City, and finally, Suttons Bay. It was originally named by Harry Chittenden Sutton, its first settler and founder in 1854.

In the spring of 1860, a party of government surveyors and their retainers began working their way from Newaygo into the pristine wilderness of northern Michigan. They were plotting the course of the Northport-Newaygo State Road, the first road into the Grand Traverse region. They were pestered along the way not by bears or wolves, as some had feared, but by mosquitoes of a size and ferocity none of them had ever seen and by snakes that slithered into their bedrolls for warmth on chilly nights.

Toward the end of their journey, after working several days in a dismal swamp, they came out at the tiny village of Suttonsburg. Here they were met by Harry Sutton and invited to dinner at his log home. After enjoying their first decent meal in weeks, they were entertained by Sutton and his wife Martha with stories of the early days at the settlement.

In the summer of 1854, Harry and Martha and their two children left their home in New York State by boat via the Erie Canal to Traverse City. Here the wife and children remained for a few days while Harry reconnoitered the area for a place to establish their new home. He chose a site on the beautiful bay that bears his name. While Sutton built the new log house with the help of an Ottawa Indian, they shared a two-room cabin with the Indian family.

Martha Sutton, age 22, had never come in contact with Indians before, and she was uneasy at first—particularly when Harry had to go to Traverse City or Northport for supplies. During his absence she would pile packing boxes against the door between the two rooms for protection. Later, however, they all became good friends. Martha was especially grateful to the Indian woman for saving the life of one of her children. One day when the child seemed near death from dysentery, she brewed a medicine from woodland herbs that soon restored the baby's health.

Sutton soon realized that their only livelihood had to come from the forest. He hired Indian helpers and set about clearing the land and selling cordwood for fuel to lake steamers. He also sold hemlock bark for use in the tanneries at Milwaukee and Chicago. His business prospered and he kept adding to his holdings. By far the busiest man in town, he doubled as self-taught shoemaker and doctor, administering to the sick by using native American remedies. It was said that his tonics were surprisingly effective, especially when combined (as most of them were) with a little corn whiskey. Sutton was also the first village school teacher. And when Suttons Bay was granted a post office of that name in 1861, he became its first postmaster.

But Harry Sutton was a restless young man, one of the many who took Greeley's advice: "Go west, young man, and grow up with the country." Even at the age of 42 (which was no longer young in those days) he still had a wanderlust and the spirit of adventure in his blood, and evidently Suttons Bay wasn't far enough west for him. Beguiled by tales of the bountiful western prairies, he sold his holdings in Suttons Bay in 1871 and with his family—except one child—boarded a lake steamer at Northport to begin the long journey. A band of Indians on ponies accompanied them to the dock and stood waving farewell until the boat was out of sight. The Suttons had been great friends of the Indians. They were sorry to see them go.

Left behind was daughter Harrietta, who had married George T. Carr a month before the family's departure. He and a man named Fox built the first sawmill at Suttons Bay in the early 1870s.

THE HERMIT OF BASSETT ISLAND

Hardly a man is still alive who remembers Dick Bassett, the Hermit of Bassett Island. Yet Dick was something of a celebrity in his day, not only in Traverse City but all over the country.

Not that Dick ever sought notoriety—far from it. Notoriety was thrust upon him.

Sometime in the 1870s or early 1880s Dick homesteaded the little island—just off the north end of Marion Island—that came to be called Bassett Island. Not much is known about his life before he came here. He refused to answer any questions about his background. It wasn't that he had anything to hide. He just figured it was nobody's business. He was probably about 30 when he came to this part of the country, a Civil War veteran looking for peace and quiet.

The place he called home is a sometimes island. Sometimes it is and sometimes it isn't, depending on the water level in Grand Traverse Bay. During high water Bassett is separated from Marion Island by a narrow channel, while in times of low water you can walk dry shod from one island to the other.

Dick was a special kind of hermit. Although he led mostly a solitary life, he wasn't anti-social. He welcomed visits from friends and even strangers, whom he entertained with his dry humor and wit. A well-educated man, he could hold his own in almost any

164

conversation. In short, he was a friendly kind of recluse—just so long as you didn't get nosey and try to pry into his past. Then he got as cold and uncommunicative as the Sphinx.

Dick fished for a living. He made a little money—enough for his modest needs—by catching and selling whitefish and lake trout. He also kept a beautiful garden and planted apple trees, some of them still standing.

Marion Island down through the years has been a haven for American Bald Eagles, and there were many eagles on the island in Bassett's time. Dick had pet names for a pair of them. He called the female "Old Hell Cat" and the male "Poor Him."

"You know, that she-eagle reminds me of a woman I almost married," Dick remarked while explaining how he named the birds. "She is the orneriest, cussedest, bossiest female I ever saw. She don't give that mate of hers no peace, and every time I see her I think about what I escaped."

"But take that male bird," he went on. "He's the feller I feel sorry for. He'll go out and catch a rabbit or a duck and bring it home. He no sooner lights in that big pine tree than the fight starts. Old Hell Cat will squawk and fret and cuss until he gives it to her and then he has to go out and find another. He only gets the leavings, poor feller."

In 1898 Dick Bassett surprised everybody by moving into Traverse City for the winter and setting up a fish market on South Union Street. That year he had a dozen men fishing for him in Grand Traverse Bay.

Shortly after this, Dick committed the ultimate betrayal of all hermits and misogynists. He got married and left town for good.

The happy couple settled in California.

DERBY HATS WERE COOL AT GOOD HARBOR

The village of Good Harbor got its start in 1868 when a veteran seaman named H. D. Pheatt chose to retire on Good Harbor Bay in northwestern lower Michigan. From boyhood he had sailed the Great Lakes for 41 years, 38 of them as shipmaster of schooners and steamers. In 1863 he built a dock on the bay and began cutting cordwood fuel for passing steamers. Five years later he built a small sawmill there, and the village of Good Harbor grew up around it.

In 1869 Pheatt sold the sawmill, bought 200 acres a mile or so down the bay, and took up farming. In 1882, he built a gristmill powered by Shetland Creek, which connects Lime Lake and Little Traverse Lake.

Meanwhile, the Good Harbor property was taken over by the Schomberg brothers, Richard, Otto, and Henry. They built a much larger sawmill and used the smaller one for a barrel factory. They harvested the big timber in the area, hiring as many as 100 teams of horses to haul the logs from the woods to the mill. Their successful operation spurred the growth and development of the village.

At the peak of its existence Good Harbor had 18 houses, a two-story boarding house, two general stores, a warehouse, a saloon, and a feed barn. In addition to the big sawmill and the barrel factory, it also had a small sawmill—built by Otto Theis of Leland—and a cheese factory south of town. It was granted a post office in 1886, with August Bartling as postmaster; the office was lodged in Richard Schomberg's general store. The town had a population of more than 300.

Dick was a shrewd businessman. On one of his buying trips to Chicago he came upon a special clearance sale of derby hats. He bought 500 of them and had them shipped to Good Harbor along with his other purchases.

Derby hats in Good Harbor? Was Dick Schomberg losing his mind?

As things turned out, though, it appeared that Dick knew very well what he was doing. He offered a derby hat free to every customer who bought at least $10 worth of merchandise in his store. (In those days $10 was worth about $100 today.)

Somehow, derby hats caught on in Good Harbor and other nearby communities. They became prized possessions. Men wore them to church on Sundays, to weddings, and on other special occasions. In contemporary slang, derby hats became cool in Good Harbor—a mark of distinction.

But good days in Good Harbor came to an end when the big sawmill burned down in 1905. After that, most of the villagers lost heart and moved away. The post office closed down in 1907, and most of the buildings stood empty until the winter of 1924, when John Peters of Leland tore them down for their lumber.

Some of the people moved to the tiny hamlet of Schomberg, a mile or two southeast of Good Harbor. Schomberg owed its existence to the Manistee & Northeastern Railroad, which built a branch to the village from its Cedar-Provemont line in 1903. It was given a post office in 1904, but lost it when the M&NE abandoned almost all of its Leelanau County lines in 1934.

Nothing is left of Good Harbor and Schomberg today.

MANSEAU AND THE OLD GRISTMILL

Manseau never got big enough to become a bona fide ghost town. But it had a siding on the old Traverse City Leelanau & Manistique Railroad, and it was a gathering place for Leelanau County farmers, who brought their grain to the gristmill for sale or to be ground for their own use.

The water-powered mill was built in 1859 by Antoine Manseau, Jr. In 1856 he had bought an acre of land on what he named Kenosha Creek from an Indian named Keywatosa for a hundred dollars. Three years later he dammed the creek, built a 26 x 30-foot mill and started grinding grain with a pair of imported millstones. They came from France and were made of buhrstone, a composite of limestone and silica widely used for grindstones in those days.

The old mill still stands on what is now called Belanger Creek, 3-1/2 miles north of Suttons Bay. It is probably the oldest grist mill in the Grand Traverse area, antedating the Norris mill in Greilickville (now a residence) by at least two or three years.

Like his father, Antoine, Sr., the younger Manseau was a millwright and carpenter. He was born in Canada, as was his father, and came to this country in 1838. After spending some time in Green Bay, Milwaukee, and North Manitou Island, the Manseaus settled at the mouth of Carp River in Leelanau County. There, Manseau helped his father build a dam and sawmill on the river, thus founding the town of Leland in 1853.

In 1882, Antoine, Jr. built a 16 x 16-foot addition to his Kenosha mill and installed a roller system necessary for milling flour. Even today, that mill would be a wonder of elaborate machinery or rollers, bolters, and screens. The grain moved six times from basement to top floor, through three stands of silk bolters and screens that separated the coarse bran and other by-products from the final fine-ground flour.

The mill was completely automatic. Only one man was needed to operate it—just to see that the grain kept moving in the right direction and to replace broken belts. There were fifty-two belts in the mill, and it was said that an experienced miller could tell by the sound which one had broken.

In 1906, the mill was bought by Eugene Belanger and operated by him and his sons Ignatius, Alexis, Luke and Edwin, until 1934. At that time very little grain was being raised in the Grand Traverse region, and the mill was closed down because business was slow and the owners didn't want to spend the money for necessary repairs. Most Michigan grist mills also shut down around that time.

Ed Belanger remembers the mill's last day. He remembers it especially well because it came close to being his last day, too. For much of that time, he and the farmer had stood on some planking over the seventeen-foot-deep water box that provided power for the mill wheel.

Ed went to a dance in Suttons Bay, and when he returned that night he found part of the concrete wall of the water box had given way and the planking on which they had stood was a hundred yards out on the bay ice.

"If it had happened during that day," Ed says, "we'd both have been goners for sure."

The mill stands empty now, but the dam on Belanger Pond is still intact. The mill is registered on the list of Michigan Historic Places.

ABOUT THE TOWNS & VILLAGES

WHAT HAPPENED TO BROWNSTOWN?

B rownstown was one of the earliest settlements of the Grand Traverse region. It started when Captain John Brown of Racine, Wisconsin—whose schooner *Phalanx* was a familiar sight on Grand Traverse Bay—bought land in 1858 in Antrim County's Torch Lake Township, which includes about half of the narrow peninsula that separates Torch Lake from Grand Traverse Bay. At one of its narrowest points, near the Indian portage between the lake and the bay, Captain Brown built a log house and barn; and the settlement grew up around Brown's homestead.

The village got a boost when it was given a post office in 1866, but the Captain wasn't there to help celebrate the event. For reasons obscure he had sold the property in 1864 to the lumbering company of Wilcox and Newell, and departed. Major Cicero Newell became postmaster on June 4th of that year, and the name of the village was changed from Brownstown to Torch Lake. (The Indian name for the lake was Waswagonink, for the flaming torches that the Indians used for lights while spearing fish at night.)

The settlers were confident that the town would become a shipping point for commerce and the Great Lakes steamers, or at least a wooding station on a par with Northport. But their hopes were blighted when Cicero Newell and L. G. Wilcox built a big sawmill and dock on the bay shore directly across from Northport (hence their name Eastport for the mill and also for a small village, originally named Wilson, at the head of Torch Lake). Eastport was only two miles north of Torch Lake village, and it had better prospects because its geographical position gave it much easier access for a potential growing market.

So that was the beginning of the end for Brownstown, though it managed to linger for a while. The final blow was the loss of its post office in 1911.

SLABTOWN AND BAGHDAD

In 1853 Perry Hannah built a big steam sawmill on Grand Traverse Bay where Clinch Park now stands. To accommodate his mill workers he also built a large boarding house at the northwest corner of Bay and Union streets near the mill. It was occupied by single young men, who incidentally outnumbered the single women by three or four to one. Later, as a hotel under the ownership of William Fowle, it became known as the Bay House.

Originally there was an open space behind the boarding house and between the Boardman River and the bay. Here a collection of one-room shanties sprang up like magic almost overnight. They were built by and for the mill workers with families. Constructed of slabs, edgings and other waste material from the mill, they were usually available free for the asking. There was one two-room shanty in the group, the residence of Perry Hannah and his wife. Jokingly, Mrs. Hannah called it the "Shanty Palace." The place itself was called Slabtown or Baghdad.

Slab cutting is the first step in squaring a log for making lumber. A slab is cut from four sides of a log to produce a single square beam of various sizes of boards. The slabs have random thicknesses and widths. Some have bark near the edges. All are considered unmarketable.

In building a slab house, the slabs are nailed vertically to the upper and lower plates of a simple box frame without studs. The interior walls were usually covered with tarpaper. Small windows were limited to one or two. With a good wood stove you could keep comfortably warm even in the dead of winter.

So that's how Slabtown got its name. But so far as Baghdad is concerned, nobody today seems to have a clue to the origin of the name. Maybe it was a joke. The ancient city of Baghdad on the Tigris River in Iraq was rich and powerful. Except that Travese City's Baghdad also lay on a river, the Boardman River, any comparison of the two must have been good for a laugh.

The boundaries of Baghdad-Slabtown were the Boardman River and West Bay from Union Street to Division Street.

TRAVERSE CITY & ELK RAPIDS:
EARLY RIVALS

In 1858 somebody wrote the editor of the *Grand Traverse Herald* newspaper, then in its first year of publication, that if Traverse City continued to grow as it had during the past few years, it would soon be as big as Elk Rapids.

Both villages started out at about the same time (early 1850's) with roughly the same advantages. Both had good geographic locations for water transportation (which was all there was at that time) and both had equally dynamic leadership—Traverse City under Perry Hannah, Elk Rapids under Wirt Dexter and Percy Noble.

During the next 30 years, Elk Rapids matched Traverse City in the number of its successful enterprises: lumbering, milling, shipping, merchandising, and banking—and went three better: chemicals, pig iron, and cement. But by 1890, Traverse City was the dominant community and Elk Rapids began to decline into the small town that it is today.

Why? The answer is the railroad.

Undoubtedly other factors were also involved, but the principal reason for the rise of Traverse City and the decline of Elk Rapids was the Grand Traverse & Indiana Railroad.

In 1869, the GR&I began inching north from Grand Rapids. Under the terms of its charter, it was required to build a railroad from Grand Rapids to some point on Traverse Bay. For this, it would receive thousands of acres of U.S. government land along the right of way as a bonus. The GR&I reached Cadillac in 1871. By that time Traverse City was astounded to learn that the railroad intended to pass them by.

Perry Hannah lost no time in doing something about it. He formed a corporation known as the Traverse City Railroad and raised $40,000 for a branch line from Walton Junction to Traverse City. It was completed in November 1872.

That did it. Traverse City got its first railroad and its growth and prosperity was assured. Elk Rapids had to wait almost 20 years for another, the Chicago & West Michigan, depending meanwhile on the declining Great Lakes shipping. By that time, Traverse City had three major railroads.

Perry Hannah had the vision of what a railroad could do for Traverse City or any such backwoods community. And that made all the difference.

By the early 1900s, Traverse City had become the major railroad hub of northern Michigan. It had four railroads: Grand Rapids & Indiana, Pere Marquette, Chicago & West Michigan, and the Traverse City, Leelanau & Marquette. All of then, alas, are gone today.

HOW TO GET TO TRAVERSE CITY

Most people don't realize how isolated Traverse City was in its early days. For more than a decade the tiny village was an outpost on the western frontier—a kind of Conradian "Heart of Darkness." For five or six months of the year, when navigation on the Great Lakes shut down for the winter, Traverse City was almost completely cut off from the outside world. And it wasn't until the 1860s that the first State Road, from Northport to Newaygo, was opened. That road, now M-37, closely followed an Indian trail.

On July 13, 1859, the *Grand Traverse Herald*, predecessor of the *Record-Eagle,* printed the following instructions to travelers:

We receive many letters from different parts of the country how people can get to Grand Traverse County? To which we reply: Those living South and East will take a steamboat at Buffalo, Cleveland or Detroit and come directly to Northport, which is situated on Grand Traverse Bay ten miles from its mouth. The fare from Buffalo to Northport is about $8 and from Detroit $5.

Those who wish to visit the western part of the county on the shore of Lake Michigan will take a steamer which will agree to land them at Glen Arbor or Leland.

Those coming from the West will take passage on one of Hannah, Lay & Co.'s vessels at Chicago, which sail regularly between that point *and Traverse City during the navigation season; or one of Dexter & Noble's vessels which will land them at Elk Rapids on the eastern shore of Grand Traverse Bay at the mouth of Elk River. The fare from Chicago by sail vessel is $5. There are small boats running regularly between Northport, Traverse City, Elk Rapids and Old Mission, which will take passengers to any point on the Bay.*

There is no land route to this place except an Indian trail, over which the mail is brought by a carrier on foot, once a week. In the winter this is our only route to the outside world. A route for a State Road has been surveyed this season, and the time is not far distant when we shall have a good thoroughfare to Grand Rapids. Editors with whom we exchange papers will confer a favor by copying the above.

THE INDIAN BURIAL MOUNDS

Who built the mounds near the courthouse grounds? Nobody knows exactly who built those burial mounds—except that they were Indians, not a different race of people as some of the early historians believed. (They couldn't help it. They were just as smart as we are but they didn't have the benefit of the 150 years of accumulated scientific knowledge that we do.)

When Horace Boardman paddled up the Boardman River in 1847 searching for a good site for the area's first sawmill, he was surprised to see the mounds. They were small compared to those of the Hopewell culture that attained a high level of civilization roughly from the second century B. C. to the fourth century A. D., along the Ohio and other great rivers of the Midwest. They were probably no more than eight or ten feet tall.

Boardman knew what they were—he had probably seen burial mounds before—but none so far north as Grand Traverse Bay.

The Traverse City mounds were situated just north of Boardman Lake along the east side of the Boardman River. They were excavated long ago and leveled; no trace remains. They contained human skeletons, probably of local Native American chiefs, and quantities of artifacts—stone tools and weapons and pottery typical of the late Woodland Period.

176

Were those mounds built by the so-called mound builders of the Hopewell culture? Probably not. They were built centuries later, but they may have been influenced by the Hopewell Indians. However, burial mounds are found all over the world; they are a common style of burial among many prehistoric people.

What happened to the Hopewell Indians? One theory is that they were the ancestors of the Iroquois, the most warlike of all the Indian nations, who had reached a high degree of political organization at the time of Columbus' "discovery" of America.

IRON WORKS AT LELAND

The Leland Iron Works had a short and troubled life, all 14 years of it, from 1870 to 1885. And after it came to an end, many people wondered if it was such a good idea, after all.

The site had several important advantages. It was only 80 miles by water to Escanaba, the main shipping point for carrying iron ore around the lakes. It had abundant maple and beech timber, essential for producing the kind of charcoal used in iron smelting. And it had ample resources of limestone, necessary to the process.

But it also had one big disadvantage. Leland has no natural harbor. In bad weather, ships sometimes had to wait days before it was safe to load or unload their cargo at the dock.

In 1879, a group of Detroit businessmen formed a corporation called the Leland Lake Superior Iron Company, and decided to build an iron furnace at the little village of Leland (population 200) in northwest lower Michigan. With a capital of $150,000 they bought most of the village land north of Carp River, as well as large tracts of heavily timbered land between Carp Lake (now Lake Leelanau) and Lake Michigan. Construction on the plant began in 1869, and it was in full production by the spring of 1871. The Iron Works stood just north of the river below the dam, on land now occupied by Leland's waterfront park. Its blast furnace stack, built of fire brick, rose 75 feet in the air; it was, by far, the tallest landmark in the village.

Adjacent to it was a large building for casting pig iron ingots and smaller buildings for supplies.

Just west of the river bend on River Street, the company built a dozen beehive-shaped charcoal kilns on the present property of the Blue Bird restaurant. The charcoal was carried to the furnace on a narrow gauge railroad, powered by horses. The river bank where Riverside Inn now stands was piled high with cordwood for the charcoal kilns, and the great pile extended south around the river bend to the company store, located between the river and the present County Courthouse. The Company operated two other sets of charcoal kilns in the vicinity of Provemont (Lake Leelanau).

The Company employed about 150 men. Most of them worked in the woods all around the lake, cutting hardwood, loading it on barges, and stacking it along the river. It was hard work: one four-foot piece of green hardwood was about all that one man could carry. The Company also paid $1.25 per cord to farmers along the lake. The production of charcoal was the company's biggest expense. At peak production, it took 150 cords of hardwood per day to feed charcoal to the voracious appetite of the blast furnace.

The Leland Iron Works continued in full production until the spring of 1872, when it became obvious to the company officers that the project was doomed to failure. Its huge overhead not only ate up all the profits, it also gobbled all the capital. He decided to throw in the towel. In June of that year, a colorful sea captain named E. B. Ward bought the property.

Ward was a ship builder, and he owned the largest fleet on the Great Lakes. His boats carried more lumber, iron ore and copper than any other single owner. In the spring of 1873, he acquired a steel-rolling mill in Wyandotte, Michigan, and from then on, the two plants worked together, the rolling mill taking all of the iron works' pig iron production.

But Captain Ward died in Detroit in 1875, and without his guidance his industrial empire seems to have collapsed overnight. The Wyandotte plant went into bankruptcy, and the Leland Iron Works changed ownership. It managed to limp along until 1885, when it was abandoned and allowed to decay. In 1895, the furnace chimney was torn down, and the bricks were sold for building material. The old county jail at Leland (still standing) was built of bricks from the furnace chimney.

In 1944, Fred Dickinson, editor of the *Leelanau Enterprise*, wrote the following in his "Short History of the Leland Iron Works":

> *Leland could not have been a very desirable place to live with the smoke and dirt of the smelter and kilns, charcoal dust and rough-and-ready operating personnel all in the heart of the village. There is little doubt that the future development of Leland was temporarily retarded during those 14 years. . . Leland did not come into its own until soon after the turn of the century, when its present fine resort development began to take place.*

That was the start of the charming little village that Leland is today.

IS LEELANAU COUNTY A LAND OF DELIGHT?

It sure is, but . . ."Leelanau" isn't an Indian word, and it doesn't mean "land of delight"—though most Leelanau people would argue that the flowery phrase is accurate enough to describe one of the most beautiful counties in the country.

There is no L sound in the Ojibwa language.

Henry Schoolcraft invented the word Leelanau. He also named 20 other counties in northern Michigan, some with authentic Indian words and some that sounded Indian but weren't. He wasn't trying to mislead anyone; he just liked the sounds of the words. Having married the half-Ojibwa daughter of an Indian princess, he was fluent in several Indian tongues.

In this particular case Schoolcraft was probably influenced by the poet Henry Wadsworth Longfellow, whose work he much admired. In Longfellow's *Myth of Hiawatha*, the heroine says, "from her baby Neenzu, she was called Leelinau." In the state records,

Leelanaw was spelled with a "w" because some clerk in Lansing mistook the handwritten "u" for a "w". This spelling was officially corrected in 1896.

Henry Rowe Schoolcraft was a Leonardo da Vinci kind of man. He was an explorer, geologist, ethnologist, and prolific writer. In 1821 he accompanied Gen. Lewis Cass as geologist on an expedition to explore northern Michigan and the upper Great Lakes. They discovered what they thought incorrectly was the source of the Mississippi River. In 1822 he was appointed Indian Agent with headquarters at Sault Ste. Marie, and began his ethnological studies. His administration as Indian Agent was later much increased and he made his headquarters at Mackinac.

Schoolcraft made another journey to the Mississippi River in 1828 and served in the territorial legislature from 1828 to 1832.

His monumental work on Indian tribes, "Historical and Statistical Information Respecting . . . the Indian Tribes of the United States" was published in six volumes from 1851-57. Schoolcraft is recognized as the chief pioneer in Indian studies.

MABEL DIDN'T MAKE IT

Mabel was typical of the many little villages in northwestern Michigan that sprung up along the railroads. They prospered for a little while, then slowly withered away and died.

The Chicago & West Michigan Railroad (later the Pere Marquette and the Chesapeake & Ohio lines) reached Traverse City in 1890, then pushed on to Charlevoix and Petoskey. Mabel got its start in 1892, when Walter Hastings built a sawmill on the site, which lies on Mabel Road, two miles east of Williamsburg. That same year, the village showed enough promise and population to be awarded a post office; Adelbert Fairbanks was its first postmaster.

During the next few years Mabel shipped large quantities of lumber, shingles, railroad ties, telephone poles, and potatoes to the outside world. At its peak, it had a sawmill, shingle mill, and a general store.

Two of the most exciting things that ever happened at Mabel were a train wreck and a record-setting artesian well. The well came first.

In 1908 Gilbert Pray hired well-drillers Gardener & Son to sink a well for his house and store. They hit artesian water at seventy feet, and it was a real gusher. The water shot up forty feet in the air, higher than the store building. Its flow was estimated at 202,677 gallons a day, enough to supply the needs of a village of more than four thousand people. The well, said to be one of the largest in Michigan, made newspaper headlines all over the state.

The train wreck happened a couple years later. On the morning of July 19, 1910, two Pere Marquette freight trains collided head-on near Mabel with such force that that one engine was telescoped into the other. One man lost his life, and five were injured in the accident.

One of the trains was an "extra", northbound from Traverse City. The other was the so-called stone train, hauling limestone from Petoskey. The stone train had been forced to "double the hill" northeast of Mabel, and after leaving part of the train at Williamsburg, engine 160 went back with the caboose to pick up the other half.

Both trains were running fast when they met on a blind curve half a mile from Mabel. Grover Hammond, a farmer who lived nearby, was standing on a hill where he could see both trains, though the engineer of each train couldn't see the other. Hammond ran forward, shouting and waving his hat. Engineer Fred Vahey of the stone train saw him and shut off the steam. At almost the same instant Frank Griffin of the "extra" caught sight of the stone train and slammed on the brakes. But it was too late—the engines collided just seconds later.

Both crews managed to jump to safety before the crash. But Walter Beeman of Elk Rapids, riding in the cab of the stone train, got caught in the wreckage and was killed. Slightly injured were engineer Paul Obenauf, conductor Edward Egan, and firemen George Jackson and John Zimmerman, both of Traverse City. Cause of the accident: misinterpreted orders.

After that, Mabel resumed its gentle drift into the mists of history. The timber petered out, and the mill shut down. Mabel lost its post office in 1913, and the general store closed soon after.

But the few people who live there still call Mabel their home, and the artesian well still flows at a strong and steady rate, filling a pond in the open foundations of the old general store and a creek that meanders across the flat. And if you sit there by the water, in the shade of a giant willow tree, you can savor something of the slow time and quiet of a bygone way of life—even though on M-72, less than a quarter mile away, people in automobiles dash by at seventy and eighty miles an hour, as if their lives depended on it.

NORTH UNITY NEARLY STARVED

If it hadn't been for some Indians and a few brave pioneers, North Unity might have become a lost colony like the one at Roanoke Island in Virginia almost three centuries earlier.

North Unity was first settled in 1855 by mostly Czech immigrants. After living a short while in Chicago, they formed an association and delegated a few men to scout the northwestern shore of Lake Michigan in a sailboat for a suitable place to start a settlement. After some time they docked at Good Harbor, a small village of French and Indians opposite the Manitou Islands.

From there they scouted west along the shore until they came to a beautiful, heavily wooded valley which was open to homesteading. It lay between Sugar Loaf Hill, which they named "Blahnik" after a famous hill in their Bohemian homeland, and what is now known as Pyramid Point. This, they decided, was the ideal place for their settlement.

They reported their find back to Chicago, and in August of 1855, several families made the move. They were the families of Anton Kucera, Charles Viskocil, Jacob Celak, Joseph Berkman, V. Jandus, Edward Kafka, N. Tabor, L. Kroupa, and two single men, Victor Petertyl and Albert Staphenek. Other families followed later in the fall of 1855. Almost all are well represented in the Grand Traverse region today.

Back in 1855 there was just enough time, before winter set in, to clear a little land near the lakeshore and build a barracks, where all of them lived for a year or two until they could stake out homestead claims. The barracks was roughly 150 feet long and 20 feet wide, with rooms partitioned off for each family.

The first winter was long and hard. Only a few of the families had brought food supplies from Chicago, and there hadn't been time or space to put in gardens. Those who had extra food shared with the others until the supply ran out and everybody began to suffer from hunger.

To make matters worse, a schooner carrying food and other supplies for the settlers ran into a storm near the Manitou Islands, and the crew, presumably to lighten the load, jettisoned all the cargo except a barrel of whiskey on which they proceeded to get roaring drunk. The ship and crew survived, suffering nothing worse than hangovers, but that didn't help the starving settlers.

They managed to barter a little corn from the Indians, but nothing else was available. Lake Michigan froze early that winter, and no other boats could get through. Finally, on the point of starvation, Francis Kraits and Victor Musil with a few other men crossed the ice to North Manitou Island with a sled and brought back several bushels of potatoes from the Islanders. This sustained them until early spring when the passenger pigeons arrived and Lake Michigan was open for navigation.

The village thrived during the next few years as more and more people moved in. It had a schoolhouse, a sawmill, and a general store. In 1859 it was awarded a post office, and John Hartung became its first postmaster. Joseph Shalda built a gristmill on the Lake Michigan outlet of the creek that bears his name.

But the settlement had a setback in 1871, when most of the village was destroyed by fire. After that, most of the settlers moved inland and dispersed, and Shalda's new general store, opposite Cleveland Township Hall, became the area's new center of activity.

NORTHWESTERN MICHIGAN COLLEGE

When and how did Northwestern Michigan College get its start? Someone has written that all you need to start a university are two people sitting on a log—a student and a teacher. When NMC first opened its doors on September 17, 1951, it had only a little more.

The idea for a college in Traverse City was the brain-child of Dr. Glen Loomis, who came here in 1838 as superintendent of schools. Soon after his arrival he invited most of Traverse City's civic leaders to a barbecue in his back yard. There, after the barbeque was over, he presented his ideas for a two-year community college as an adjunct to the Traverse City school system. He said he had been in touch with some of Michigan's best people in the education field, and they all agreed that his plan was very feasible.

Loomis' plan met with great enthusiasm from his guests at the barbeque, and before long they formed a corporation for the promotion and development of such a college. Among them, to name just a few, were Les Beiderman, who built the first radio station here in 1940; Preston Tannis, the college's first president; Arnell Engstrom, Chairman of the powerful Ways & Means Committee in Lansing; Merle Lutz, Executive Secretary of the Chamber of Commerce; and of course, Glen Loomis.

A problem arose during one of the early board meetings. According to Loomis' plan, the college would become an extension of the Traverse City schools, and of course under his supervision as superintendent of schools. Les Beiderman voiced strong opposition to this concept. Loomis' plan was fatally flawed, Beiderman said. The college must stand on its own two feet, a separate entity, not connected in any way to the schools.

The battle was joined and both went at it hot and heavy. Both were ambitious strong-minded men with sizeable egos. Each presented cogent arguments for his own point of view. In the end, Beiderman won the day. It wasn't only that Beiderman could talk faster than Loomis, but also that, at least in the minds of the majority of the board, Beiderman was right.

In the spring of 1951, the Michigan Legislature—under the legal guidance of Harry Running and the legislative skill of Arnell Engstrom—passed a bill creating a new concept in higher education: a two-year regional or community college. Traverse City's Northwestern Michigan College was the first such college in Michigan.

It opened its doors on September 17, 1951, with an enrollment of 65 students and six teachers, headed by President Preston Tannis. Its first classrooms were in the city-owned airport terminal building, which had been headquarters of the U. S. Coast Guard's Traverse City unit during the war. The college was moved to the first building on its pine-shaded campus in 1956.

SLEEPING BEAR

Is the Sleeping Bear Dune the largest moving sand dune in the world?

According to Don McNew of Glen Arbor, who has made a life-long study of sand dunes, Sleeping Bear is by no means the world's tallest, and it doesn't move very much.

McNew points out that the Sleeping Bear Dune complex is perched on a base of gravelly hills thrown up along the lakeshore by the last continental glacier. Sleeping Bear Dune itself is not more than 200 feet high, and probably not more than 150 feet. (A true sand dune is composed of nothing but sand; the glacial hills don't qualify.) Thus, Sleeping Bear is dwarfed by the Great Sand Dunes of Colorado which up to 500 feet, and by the dunes in the deserts of north Africa and the Middle East, which approach 900 feet tall.

McNew also points out another misconception. To say that Sleeping Bear is moving or shifting is rather meaningless, since most sand dunes shift to some extent, he says.

"Plant cover, wind direction and intensity, and human activity all cause sand movement to vary from place to place, and from year to year. However, the amount of shifting at Sleeping Bear can be measured in feet per year, while the movement of certain dunes in desert regions of Asia and Africa is measured in feet per day!"

Another popular misconception is that the shifting sands of Sleeping Bear will eventually fill in Little Glen Lake.

Actually, the wind-blown sand from the dunes is carried not to the east but to the northeast, toward Sleeping Bear Point, not Little Glen Lake. This is due to the great southwesterly gales off Lake Michigan. Uncle Sam found that out when he established a Coast Guard Station at the Point in 1901. Thirty years later, the station had to be moved a half mile east along the beach because blowing sand threatened to bury the buildings.

The movement of sand at the Dune Climb is mainly due to human activity, McNew says. Every time people climb the dune, sand is pushed down behind them. What actually happens is that the dune is being flattened by millions of human feet over the years. Just a few decades ago, the dune was reported to be over 150 feet tall, but the latest measurement shows that it has shrunk to 130 feet.

All this is in no way to belittle Sleeping Bear Dune's great natural beauty and charm. As millions of visitors from this country and, indeed, all over the globe will attest, it is one of nature's great wonders of the world.

THE BAPTIST RESORT

One of the most popular summer resorts in the area at the beginning of the 20th Century was Traverse Beach. It was popularly known as the Baptist Resort because of the church affiliation of its founders, a group of Chicago businessmen. The resort comprised more than 100 wooded acres in Elmwood Township two miles north of Traverse City on what is now called West Bayshore Road. It had almost a mile of frontage on both Grand Traverse Bay and Cedar Lake.

Opened in 1892, Traverse Beach offered its guests a wide variety of indoor and outdoor activities—swimming, boating, fishing, lawn tennis, bowling and croquet—as well as food and lodging. The mammoth hotel had 45 rooms, an 80-foot-long dining room, and a big kitchen and recreation parlor. The resort met all lake steamers and trains with its horse-drawn omnibus.

Hotel rooms were priced from $10 to $14 a week. Guests could dine on Mackinac trout and other house specialties for 50 cents a meal, children half-price. Electric bells connected each room with the office. The beds had horse-hair mattresses and steel springs. There were bathrooms on all three floors and a hot bath could be arranged at "trifling expense." Its brochure also boasts two mineral springs, one containing iron, the other sulphur; their tonic effect, it claims, is "quite apparent."

Like Neahtawanta and Edgewater resorts on Old Mission Peninsula, Traverse Beach was a family resort, with the emphasis on family. It was customary, for example, for mother and the kids to spend a week, two weeks, or even all summer at a northern Michigan resort, while poor old dad might join them for a week's vacation or maybe only an occasional weekend when he could get away. The Pennsylvania and Pere Marquette railroads both ran daily "resort specials", big trains pulled by two locomotives. In those pre-auto and pre-motel days, the summer resorts did a big business.

In addition to vacation facilities, Traverse Beach offered real estate opportunities. Lots on the property sold for $100 to $200. The owners platted most of the acreage and laid out a network of connecting roads that still exist. So does part of the old hotel with its distinctive twelve gables (now only eight). The front half, facing the road, was torn down in the 1930s, and the other half, on the steep west bank, was remodeled into apartments.

Unfortunately, Traverse Beach had an unusually short life. By reasons of "financial embarrassment" it closed its doors in 1906. A few members of the old Chicago families still spend at least part of the summer in their own old cottages.

THE JAY P. SMITH WALKWAY

When did the Jay P. Smith Walkway come into being? Was there always a gap at 131 East Front Street between two buildings?

No. The gap is of comparatively recent origin.

In 1881, Julius Huellmantel, a successful merchant tailor who lived in the splendid Gothic house at Cass and Ninth Streets, built a commercial wooden building at 131 East Front. It was known henceforth as the Huellmantel Block. In 1883 he rented the street-level shop to E. W. Hastings, who sold sewing machines and musical instruments.

In 1883, Huellmantel sold the building to J. G. Johnston, who turned it into a drugstore. The Johnson Drugstore remained in business until 1895, when the property was taken over by A. A. McCoy, who sold fruit and oysters and, later, candy and produce. The upper floor was occupied by Nora Nichols and Ellathine Smith, who ran a boarding house. In 1902, the shop below was turned into a restaurant, Edward A Payne, proprietor. In 1902, there were two shops at street level: George M. Gilbert, tailor, and the Eureka Café.

In 1915, Joseph Klassen opened a shop there called The Shoe Market, and in 1948 it became the Busy Bee Restaurant.

The rickety old building was torn down in the early 1950s, and 131 East Front Street became a vacant lot until some time in the late 1950s or early 1960s, when the lot was purchased by the City.

On Monday, Mar. 1, 1965, the City Commission passed the following resolution: That the property acquired by the City for a walkway from Front Street to the footbridge across the Boardman River be named the Jay P. Smith Walkway in honor and in appreciation of the services rendered to this community by the late Jay P. Smith. Motion by Chase, supported by Stulen. Present were: Dr. Robert H. Chase, Ralph R. Pulcipher, Kenneth Lindsay, George A. Gilbert, Carter B. Strong, Frank L. Stulen, and Dr. John G. Milliken.

Jay P. Smith worked for the *Traverse City Record Eagle* from 1921 until his retirement in 1961. A great editor and civic leader, Smith was a native of Traverse City and knew where all the bodies were buried. He and prominent writer/orchardist Harold Titus were the founders of the National Cherry Festival. Smith died on December 23, 1962.

TIN CAN CORNERS AND CAMP FIVE

Fifty years ago most Traverse City people were familiar with Tin Can Corners—where it is and how it got its name. Now only a few remember.

Tin Can Corners lies on the pine plains south and east of Traverse City. Take Supply Road (used long ago to carry supplies to the lumber camps) to its junction with Hobbs Highway. Then continue on Supply Road for about three miles. There you will come upon a sandy crossroad called Strombolus Road to the north and Muncie Lake Road to the south. That's Tin Can Corners.

Strombolus Road leads north to Camp Five (what's left of it), one of the largest of the Hannah, Lay & Company's lumber camps. It lies about two miles north of Supply Road, just beyond Strombolus Lake (formerly called Perch Lake). A big granite boulder marks the campsite. Look around and you'll find traces of the foundations of the bunkhouse and cook shanty. Years ago, Traverse City State Bank installed a bronze plaque on the face of the boulder, commemorating the history of Camp Five. The boulder is still there, but the plaque is gone. Some thief pried it loose from the rock, and it was never replaced.

In the early 1870s the lumberjacks at Camp Five began to cut the last big stand of white and Norway (red) pine in the Boardman River basin. It took them over ten years to finish the job.

In his book *Vinegar Pie* Al Barnes wrote about some of the characters who worked at Camp Five. One was a big, good-natured hulk of a man whom the foreman called Eric the Swede because nobody knew his last name. He had only one arm but he could out-chop and out-saw almost any other man in the camp. The only money he drew one winter in the early 1880s was enough to buy tobacco, felt boots, and a little whiskey for "medicinal" purposes.

Some time later, though, he borrowed five dollars from one of the crew and headed for Traverse City. There, it was later reported, he got uproariously drunk in the saloons and was never seen here again—not even to pick up his personal belongings at the camp.

"Somewhere in the old Hannah, Lay & Company books," Al Barnes wrote, "there is a cash balance due to Eric the Swede."

So how did Tin Can Corners get its name?

Fifty years ago, Tin Can Corners was a favorite gathering place for hunters in the fall and picnickers in the summer. At that time there were half a dozen old logging roads between Hobbs Highway and Tin Can Corners, and most of them led to Camp Five. None of them, including Supply Road, was paved or identified by name or number. So, to avoid confusion, people decided to put up some kind of marker at the crossroads. They hung strings of empty tin cans on a tree to mark the spot. And that's how Tin Can Corners got its name.

ARTSIAN WELLS

At a depth of 250 to 400 feet beneath the Traverse City area there is a layer of porous limestone between layers of impervious rock. This huge aquifer holds countless millions of gallons of spring water under pressure. In the years between 1882—when the first artesian well was sunk on the State Hospital grounds—and the early 1900s—when the city started pumping its water supply from the bay—artesian wells supplied water for many Traverse City residences and business establishments.

The State Hospital well was drilled to a depth of some 300 feet and supplied over 60,000 gallons per 24-hour day. A new 12-inch well, drilled in the 1950s to 410 feet, supplied some 800,000 gallons a day.

The first well in town was sunk around 1890 by E. L. Ransome for his home at 420 E. Front Street. After drilling 271 feet he was rewarded by a steady flow of ice-cold water of great purity. His two-inch well supplied about 100,000 gallons per day.

A four-inch well at the High School was drilled a year or two later to a depth of 275 feet. It had a flow of almost 300,000 gallons and a head of 48 feet. It was piped all through the school building and grounds, where a public drinking trough was visited daily by dozens of horses. It was said that the horses seemed to prefer this water to any other, and refused to drink anything else!

The largest well in town was completed in 1895 at the rear of the City Opera House on Front Street. It was 335 feet deep, with a head of 58 feet, and the six-inch pipe produced 400,000 gallons a day. It was also piped into the Friedrich, Wurzburg, Lautner, and Greilick buildings.

Egbert Ferris's well on State Street was 333 feet deep and flowed at a daily rate of 120,000 gallons. It supplied the European Horse Hotel and a number of private residences.

The Park Place Hotel well was 307 feet deep, with a four-inch pipe and a 19-foot head. It was used exclusively for the hotel and its grounds. Its flow was measured at 148,000 gallons.

The Terrace Lawn Artesian Well Company had a well on Washington Street 300 feet deep with a four-inch pipe. It had a head of 13 feet and a flow of 24,000 gallons. The company was formed by property owners in the Washington-Boardman vicinity and piped throughout the block. Later, another well was sunk by Ferris back of his house at 622 Washington.

A well on the old county fairgrounds was 237 feet deep. Originally it had a flow of 80,000 gallons, but it rose only eight feet above ground level—so it was driven deeper to get more flow and elevation.

Perry Hannah's well on Sixth Street was 257 feet deep with a head of 44 feet and a flow of 120,000 gallons. Later, another well was driven within a few feet of it.

Dentist T. Walter Thirlby had a well at his house on Sixth Street, and the water was also piped to several other houses and to Shilson & Brezina's store and the Boardman River House on Union Street. It was 237 feet deep and had a 45-foot head.

One of the last wells driven in the 1890s was that of Wilhelm Brothers men's store on the corner of Eighth Street and Union. It was 357 feet deep, with a 45-foot head and a flow of 72,000 gallons. This well and others, including a water fountain on the southeast corner of Front and Union, were still flowing in later years when, for various reasons, they were plugged or capped.

The most recent wells to be capped were one at Jerry Oleson's original store on West Front Street, and one on the bay shore just south of the Marathon dock in Greilickville.

Artesian water in the Traverse City area gets its pressure from the subterranean flow of water deep down from the glacial hills that flank the area on three sides.

BLACKWOOD

Remember Blackwood? Hardly anyone does. The name of a tiny village nine miles southwest of Traverse City didn't last long enough to stick in people's memory. It was in the late 1870s or early 1880s when a man named James B. Blackwood platted and recorded the village, and gave it his name. That was his privilege, since he owned a majority of the lots in the original plat. Little else is known about the man.

But when the Chicago & West Michigan Railroad came through in 1890, they renamed the Blackwood location Grawn Station. And the name was shortened to Grawn when the village was given a post office in 1890. William H. Gibbs was its first postmaster.

Grawn was the name of the village's most prominent citizen, Professor Charles T. Grawn. Before moving to the Traverse City area Professor Grawn resigned his position as superintendent of State Normal School at Mt. Pleasant in 1884 to become superintendent of Traverse City Schools, a position he filled for 13 years. He was also the maternal grandfather of Michigan Governor William G. Milliken.

By 1905 Grawn was on its way to becoming a fairly good sized town. It had two sawmills, shingle mill, barber shop, drugstore, three general stores, a produce company, hardware store, saloon, millinery shop and a big two-story hotel. Its population was about 300, and still growing.

Today Grawn still has its post office, and many of the old houses within the original plat are still inhabited. But over time, it has lost its identity as an integrated community. It has no shopping facilities or industries and by some standards it qualifies as a bona-fide ghost town, swallowed up by Traverse City.

The old hotel still stands on the corner of State and Brook Streets, but it's empty now, dilapidated and devoid of paint. The building's last tenant ran a small grocery and liquor store; he closed its doors at least 20 years ago; it was the last commercial enterprise in town. Next to it lies another deserted wooden building, the old blacksmith and livery stable.

The last Chesapeake & Ohio passenger train passed by the town on Saturday morning, October 29, 1966. Hardly anyone was around to wave goodbye.

BRIEF HISTORY OF TRAVERSE CITY AND ENVIRONS

Most northern Michigan towns grew up around a sawmill—pine lumber gave them birth. Traverse City was no exception. It got started in 1847, when Captain Harry Boardman, a prosperous farmer near Naperville, Illinois, bought 200 acres of virgin pine timber at the foot of Grand Traverse Bay and furnished his son, Horace, with the means to build a sawmill there. Horace and two or three hired hands sailed north from Chicago in his father's sloop, *Lady of the Lake*, and arrived on the site in early June.

With the help of local Indians they finished the sawmill in October of that same year. It stood on the small creek (successively known as Mill Creek, Asylum Creek, and Kids Creek) that empties into the Boardman River at its western loop on Wadsworth Street. The only other settlement in the vast wilderness for miles around was an Indian mission near the tip of the peninsula that separates the arms of Grand Traverse Bay. The mission had been established in 1839 by a Presbyterian missionary, Reverend Peter Dougherty.

The little Boardman mill continued to operate through the winter of 1850-51, but the results were disappointing. With its single muley saw, the mill was slow and inefficient, and when the price of pine lumber plummeted in 1850, Captain Boardman (the military title was honorary) decided to sell. He found a buyer in the newly organized Chicago lumber firm of Hannah, Lay & Company and its three youthful partners—Perry Hannah, Albert Tracy Lay, and James Morgan. Eager to develop their own timber resources, Hannah and William Morgan (brother of James) accompanied Captain Boardman to Grand Traverse Bay aboard the schooner *Venus* in the spring of 1851 and closed the deal. For $4,500 Hannah, Lay & Company acquired the sawmill and several small buildings, and the 200 acres upon which Traverse City now stands.

It is said that Captain Boardman was astonished upon arrival to find the mill shut down and all hands playing cards. Horace's explanation that he'd given his men the day off because of a threat of rain convinced the Captain that his decision to sell the property was wise.

The Hannah, Lay company lost no time in building a much larger steam mill on the Bay just west of the river's mouth. Over the next 35 years it would harvest more than 400 million board feet of pine lumber in the Boardman River valley. The lumber was shipped to company headquarters in Chicago in the company's own bottoms (sailing schooners)—some of it was used to help rebuild Chicago after the Great Fire of 1871—and great wealth flowed into the pockets of all four partners. (William Morgan had been added to the partnership in 1852.)

For the first few years Hannah and Lay alternated every six months as company head in Chicago and in Traverse City, but after 1855 Hannah took sole charge of affairs in Traverse City and Tracy Lay remained in the Windy City.

The village was laid out by Tracy Lay in 1852, and was granted a post office in 1853. During the winter the mail was carried weekly from Manistee in a backpack by an Indian called Old Joe. The first school was established in 1853 with 15-year-old Helen Goodale, daugher of Traverse City's first physician David C. Goodale, as teacher. The school was housed in a little log shanty, formerly a stable, on the south side of Front Street, just east of Boardman Avenue.

The first road south, the Northport-Newaygo State Road, was opened in 1864, closely following an old Indian trail. That helped some, but Traverse City's big breakout was the coming of the first railroad, the Grand Rapids & Indiana, on November 15, 1872. Whistles blew and church bells rang and people danced in the street. "Out of the Woods at Last", trumpeted the *Grand Traverse Herald* in banner headlines.

Henry D. Campbell, who had established the first stagecoach lines in the 1860s, built Traverse City's first big hotel, the Park Place, in 1873. The city became a railroad center with the coming of the Chicago & West Michigan in 1890 and the Manistee & Northeastern in 1892. It was incorporated as a village in 1881, and as a city in 1895, Perry Hannah elected president of both. Even during his lifetime Hannah was called "The Father of Traverse City." City water, electricity, and gas line were established by Henry D. Campbell in the late 1880s and 1890s. The population reached almost 10,000 in 1890—a ten year gain of 116%.

But dark clouds had already begun to gather on the horizon. Pine timber was depleted by 1895, and by 1915 so were the hardwoods. Also in decline were the city's mainstay industries based on wood and wood products. Its largest employer, Oval Wood Dish Company, for example, pulled up stakes in 1916 and moved to Tupper Lake, New York, taking with it at least 100 worker families and plunging the area into an economic decline that lasted until World War II, when the town seemed empty with all its young men gone, some of whom died in battle and were gone forever.

Traverse City actually lost population in the 1920s and stagnated in the 1930s. The city was partly sustained during this period by the Northern Michigan Asylum (later called Traverse City State Hospital) under its legendary superintendent Dr. James Decker Munson. It has been established in 1881. Over the course of the next 70 years the hospital employed an average of 1,000 people while caring for an estimated 50,000 patients.

But the seeds of resurgence had been sown as early as the 1890s, when the first commercial fruit farms were established and summer people from downstate Michigan, Ohio, and Illinois began to spend their vacations at resorts on Grand Traverse Bay and the inland lakes. Tourism and fruit farming led the way to Traverse City's phenomenal growth during the last half of the 20th Century, making it the "World's Cherry Capital" with its annual National Cherry Festival, and one of the nation's prime tourist attractions.

Over time Traverse City has also become northern Michigan's center for medical care, communications, banking, insurance, government and legal services, which, along with its spectacular natural beauty, have made it one of the most desirable places in the country to live.

Now, faced with accelerated growth and development, it has become the primary task of its people to keep it that way.

ENCHANTED ISLANDS, NORTH AND SOUTH MANITOU

An element of mystery hangs over the Manitou Islands, southern-most of the great archipelago that curves down from Beaver Island and its satellite sisters in the north. Home to some of the earliest settlers in the Grand Traverse region, the Manitous nevertheless remain the most primitive, unspoiled, least challenged by time and the hand of man

Chippewa and Ottawa Indians visited the islands from the earliest times but had no permanent campgrounds there; they believed the islands were haunted, sacred to the Great Spirit. They were followed by French traders and explorers looking for the Great Passage to the Western Sea.

The first permanent white settlers came with the rapid growth of Great Lakes shipping in the 1830s. The islands at first became fueling stations for the wood burning lake steamers. A man named Barton built a dock on South Manitou in 1839 and sold wood to passing steamers at $1.75 per four-foot cord. Nicholas Pickard established a wooding station on North Manitou in 1846.

The first lighthouse was built in 1839 on South Manitou. A wooden structure, it was replaced in 1858 by the one now standing on South Manitou, the oldest and tallest on the Great Lakes. It was abandoned around 1920, as was the lighthouse on North Manitou. Ships are now guided through the narrow and dangerous Manitou Passage by the automatic light station known as "The Crib", which stands near the channel in 21 feet of water.

The Manitou Passage is a ships' graveyard. More than 50 ships are known to have foundered off South Manitou alone—the latest being the *Morazon*, driven ashore in 1962 by a storm and now abandoned near the south beach. Years ago, the islanders told visitors that in the old days they could live year around on salvage from wrecked vessels.

For a short time the island economy grew and prospered. Villages sprung up, wharves were built, and a logging railroad laid out. The lumber town of Crescent on the west side of North Manitou at one time boasted a post office, saloon, hotel and one-room school. Farming followed wooding, especially on South Manitou, and the island population increased to a peak of more than 300 at the turn of the century.

But Great Lakes shipping suffered a sharp decline after 1900, and the islands were gradually isolated and almost deserted. Now only two families on South Manitou make their home there year around.

Of unusual interest is the Valley of the Giants, an ancient forest near the southeast corner of South Manitou. It contains several giant cedar trees more than 500 years old, including the National Champion White Cedar, with a girth of 206 inches and a height of 110 feet. (It toppled in a storm just recently.) Also found here are several rare species of ferns: northern holly, Braun holly, green spleenwort, and walking fern. An old cemetery lies inland from Gull Point, the graves enclosed by sharp-pointed palisade fences, the gravestones too weathered to be legible.

Both islands are now part of the Sleeping Bear Dunes National Lakeshore. A regularly scheduled ferry service provides daily transportation from Leland to both islands during the navigation season.

FIFE LAKE HAD TWO NAMES

In the beginning, Fife Lake had two parts, separate but continuous. Both were platted the same year, 1872, on the west shore of Fife Lake in the southwest corner of Grand Traverse County.

The north part, called North Fife Lake, was platted by Thomas Bates, who had bought the property from his uncle, Morgan Bates. The south part, called Fyfe Lake, was platted by John E. Shaw and others, from Grand Rapids. (The discrepancy in the names was the result of a spelling error.)

All this was done in anticipation of the arrival of the Grand Rapids & Indiana Railroad. Indeed, the village owed its existence to the GR&I.

From the beginning, a growing rivalry existed between the two towns. The railroad built its depot in north town, after a strong fight over its location. But the depot burned down shortly thereafter, suddenly and mysteriously. (North Fife Lake had its suspicions, but the case was never solved.) Just as suddenly a new depot was built in south town.

All this nonsense finally became moot in 1889, when the two settlements were consolidated as the Village of Fife Lake.

Meanwhile, the settlement got off to a flying start. Several lots in both plats were sold and occupied even before the GR&I arrived on September 1. James Monteith built the first house in Fife Lake. Chauncey Bailey bought the first lot in North Fife Lake and built a general store on it with lumber he carted from the Hannah, Lay mill in Traverse City, 21 miles away. He and his brother established a string of lumber camps on the Manistee River seven miles from Fife Lake—the first camps that far upriver at the time.

In July the Thompson brothers built the first sawmill, and it was in operation in early August. The first log to go through the mill took 38 minutes to cut up, and it yielded 600 board feet of lumber. Most of the mill's early production went into the building of the first hotel, Lake View House, a two-story structure overlooking the railroad depot and the lake.

By 1882, ten years later, the town had five general stores, two drugstores, four hotels, three millinery shops, two tobacco and liquor stores, a dry goods and clothing store, furniture store, printing office, jewelry store, restaurant, barber shop, two large sawmills, planning mill, shingle mill, and many other businesses. It also had two churches and nine saloons.

But with the end of the lumbering industry in Michigan in the early 1900s, the village went into a slow but steady decline. It suffered another blow in 1950, when the GR&I discontinued its passenger service. Population figures mark the village's slide. At its peak in 1882, Fife Lake had an estimated 1,000 people. In 1902, down to 749; in 2003, only 494.

In 1903, Fife Lake was the scene of the three final murders by a serial killer. From 1887 to 1903, at Alpena, Grayling and Fife Lake, Mary McKnight killed at least a dozen people—men, women and children—with strychnine. Almost all of her victims were close family relatives. She pleaded innocence but was found guilty of first degree murder and served 18 years of a life sentence (five members of the jury held out for several hours for a verdict of not guilty by reason of insanity) before being paroled. Years later, one member of the family explained: "Mary loved to go to a funeral."

HOW CHUM'S CORNERS GOT ITS NAME

In 1865, a young man named David E. Crandall came to the Traverse area from Wisconsin, where for five years he had been engaged in rafting logs on the Wisconsin and Mississippi Rivers. He found a job at the Gibbs Brothers sawmill at Mayfield, and worked there for eight years. He was a hard-working, likable man, and he saved his money.

On Christmas Day in 1876, he married his Wisconsin sweetheart, and they started a family of two girls and two boys, one of whom they named Deronda. (Nobody now knows why they chose that unusual name.)

Meanwhile, Crandall decided to go into the lumber business. He and his brother James formed a partnership and built a shingle mill at Grawn. After many years, the partnership was dissolved, and David took over the business with his son Deronda, whom since his childhood everybody had called "Chum." In addition to the shingle mill they also operated a big sawmill. The firm was known as D. E. Crandall & Son.

The business grew and prospered for at least 20 years, but then the big timber petered out and the lumbering industry fell on hard times.

"It was the Great Depression," says Deronda's son Max Crandall. "The Depression wiped him out." Max is the founder of Traverse City's oldest on-going home appliance business, Max's Service, now in its third generation of ownership.

Chum Crandall didn't let the Depression get him down. In 1934, he and his wife Eva bought forty acres at the junction of M-31 South and M-37, about six miles south of Traverse City, and built a house (both highways were just two-lane gravel roads at that time). A little later they added to the house a small grocery store and filling station, and named it "Chum's Corners."

Chum died in 1956, but Eva lived to be 104. In an interview in the 1980s, she told the story.

"It was just a little eight-by-eight shack with two gas pumps outside. But people started coming in from all over the area. Chum was such a friendly man. He loved people and they loved him. They called him Chum, and I was Mrs. Chum.

In the early days we had the only radio around, and all the farmers would come in and listen to boxing. And the people who came to their cottages . . . the men would fish in the morning and the women would come and visit me, and at night the men would come to visit Chum. Chum's Corners got to be a kind of gathering place."

She said that people from as far away as Buckley and Kingsley would come to buy gas because Chum always gave a sucker to all the kids. How did Chum get his nickname?

"The workers at his father's sawmills took a liking to him and called him 'Little Chum,'" Eva said. "And it just stuck."

Curley Crandall, Chum's oldest son, remembered that Chum's Corners was a bus stop, the only stop between Traverse City and Kingsley. "It was in their schedule," Curley said. "The bus stopped there twice a day."

Curley himself owned and operated a filling station, Crandall's Super Service, on the southeast corner of Eighth and Union Streets.

Chum's Sinclair Service station structure was torn down in 1970, but the junction is still called Chum's Corners.

By the way, if you had a name like Deronda, wouldn't you rather be called something else?

HOW DID TRAVERSE CITY GET ITS NAME?

Before the white man came, the Indians called it We-que-tong, meaning Head of the Bay. And even in its earliest days people began to call the tiny sawmill town Grand Traverse City because of its location at the head of Grand Traverse Bay.

In 1852, the village petitioned Washington for a post office. They asked that it be called Grand Traverse City. But the post office people had a problem with that. They pointed out that the area already had a post office named Grand Traverse. It was the name of Rev. Peter Dougherty's Indian mission on Old Mission Peninsula. Having two post offices with nearly the same name would cause a lot of confusion, they said. So why not drop the word Grand and simply call it Traverse City? And so it was done.

But that begs the question: how did Grand Traverse get its name? It comes from La Grande Traverse, which is French for The Great Crossing. It was part of the route that the Indians and the early French explorers took in traveling the east shore of Lake Michigan.

They traveled in birch bark canoes. They had to hug the shoreline because their frail craft wasn't designed for rough open water. Their lives would be endangered on the unprotected waters of Lake Michigan.

La Grande Traverse was actually a short cut. It crossed the mouth of Grand Traverse Bay from Norwood in Charlevoix County to Northport in Leelanau County. The distance is only about ten miles. The Indians were great weathermen; they had to be. When the lake was rough they waited for good weather before making this crossing. That way, they were exposed to the danger of rough waters for only a short time.

The Indians also used another short cut. It was called La Petite Traverse, which is French for The Little Crossing. It crossed the mouth of Little Traverse Bay near Petoskey.

BIGGEST LITTLE TOWN IN MICHIGAN: THOMPSONVILLE

In 1901, the village of Thompsonville in Benzie County was pushing out its chest and flexing its muscles and calling itself the "Biggest Little Town in Michigan". That was the title of a promotional booklet put out by the Thompsonville Improvement Association.

Some of the boasting was typical booster bombast, destined to lure more settlers to the backwoods community. But a lot of it was genuine. the people of Thompsonville really believed that their town was destined to become the metropolis of the north.

And why not? In the ten years since its birth, the town had grown to 1,200 people. Forty-eight shops lined both sides of Main Street. It had two hotels, three saloons, a bakery, two churches, a weekly newspaper, and a four-room schoolhouse with an enrollment of 300 pupils. It also had two sawmills, a cooperage factory, charcoal kilns for the production of pig iron, a chemical plant, handle factory, three blacksmiths and carriage shops, a bank, and a cigar factory.

The town was founded in 1890 by a half-dozen heirs of Sumner S. Thompson of Massachusetts and the Reverend Henry Ward Beecher of Boston. Before the village was incorporated in 1893, the southwest side was known as Beecher. Thompsonville was strategically situated at the junction of the Pere Marquette and the Ann Arbor railroads—121 miles north of Grand Rapids, 27 miles southwest of Traverse City, and 23 miles southeast of Frankfort. The promotional booklet called it "the most pleasant and most favored spot for a prosperous town in all the great expanse of Michigan's great peninsula."

Prospective settlers were assured that good land was available for $2 to $10 an acre, depending on location. There was a good market for logs and firewood at good prices; what was left could be sold to the charcoal kilns. Most of the land had enough standing timber to pay for and fence it when cleared.

The editor of the local weekly newspaper declared:

I call to mind a young man who four years ago contracted to buy what we call stumpland. As capital to start with, he had good health, a young wife with sound judgment, and a team of horses partly paid for. Today he has forty acres cleared, comfortable farm buildings—put up a new barn this year—, is out of debt and in five more years, if no bad luck intervenes will be independent for the rest of his days.

It all sounded pretty rosy, and the people of Thompsonville faced the new century with confidence. They were convinced that a bright future lay in store for them.

Alas, they were wrong. Thompsonville had no real future at all. Within five years the sawmills had cut all the available timber, and the charcoal kilns had gobbled up all of the rest. The bare and ravaged land was as desolate as a moonscape. Farming was unproductive: the thin, sandy sooil was so poor that it was depleted after two or three crops of potatoes. The area didn't offer much for tourists either. They passed it for the scenic lake country to the north and east.

The final blow came with the abandonment of the railroads in the 1940s and '50s. This put the town in a backwash, miles from the nearest highway.

Population figures tell the story:

1900—1200 people;
1910—815;
1920—410;

1950—313;
1980—312;
1990—265.

A few houses and empty buildings remain, but in almost every sense of the word, Thompsonville is a ghost town today.

TRAINS, SHIPS & AUTOMOBILES

EMPIRE & SOUTHEASTERN RAILROAD

Empire & Something Else" and "Empire Slow & Easy" were affectionate names bestowed on their railroad, the Empire & Southeastern, by the townspeople of Empire in southeastern Leelanau County. Like many railroads in northern Michigan, the E&SE started out as a logging railroad operating on standard gauge track; later it also carried passengers.

Around 1888, the Thomas Wilce Company of Chicago, a firm that specialized in hardwood flooring, bought a strip of land on Lake Michigan just north of the village of Empire, built a sawmill at the south end of South Bar Lake, and began lumbering operations in the surrounding timber.

The Wilce Company had been founded by Thomas Wilce, and in 1888 its management was taken over by his three sons, Thomas, Jr., George, and Harvey. Harvey came to Empire from Chicago and took over the lumber operation here, which became known as the Empire Lumber Company.

About 1890, soon after the mill was in operation, the company started to build a railroad into its timber holdings. Meanwhile, it had ordered a locomotive, rails, and flatcars from Manistee, and the mill began turning out thousands of railroad ties. The engine was hauled across the snow from Manistee on a big horse-drawn sleigh; the rails and flatcars were shipped in by boat.

After the course of the railroad had been staked out to the east, groups of workers began work on the railroad grade, using teams of horses and scrapers to level off hillocks and fill in the low spots. Flatcars loaded with ties and rails followed, and a small section of the railroad was completed each day. It went two miles due east from Empire, then made a leisurely swing to the south.

The railroad construction boss was an Irishman by the name of Dailey. His first name was Erastus, so of course everyone called him "Rat." With a blithe disregard for property rights, Dailey ran into trouble by pushing the railroad grade onto private property, in order to avoid a steep hill to the east. The property owner, Richard Ghering, discovered the trespass and angrily ordered the construction crew off his property. Dailey offered to buy rights of way, but Ghering said nothing doing. So Dailey was forced to back up a quarter of a mile and make a cut over the hill, which came to be known as Main Top. The short grade on Ghering's property is still visible today.

As it turned out, Dailey found some consolation for his error when a large spring was uncovered near the top of the hill, and water ran down to the tracks. A water tank was installed there, and it became a convenient place for the engine to take on water after its strenuous climb up the hill.

The first stretch of the railroad to be completed was from Empire to Jacktown, a distance of about six miles. Later, a five-mile branch was built to Pearl Lake. Around 1901, the main line was extended six miles to Empire Junction, where it connected with a branch line from Honor of the Manistee & Northeastern. Pete Stormer, boss of the logging operations, had lumber camps at Stormer, Peterville and Pearl Lake.

At about that time, the company bought a larger locomotive, a passenger coach, and a caboose, and began to carry passengers on a regular schedule from Empire to Empire Junction, with stops at Stormer, Peterville, Jacktown, Hill Top, and East Empire.

In 1915, most of the timber had been logged off, and in 1916 the sawmill burned down, but the passenger train continued to run until 1920. Then, in the spring of 1921, the locomotives, flatcars, and caboose were sold to a Manistee company. The rails were taken up, loaded on the flatcars, and hauled away.

Nobody wanted the passenger coach. It sat for several years on a short section of track near Jacktown, then disappeared. Thieves working at night dismantled the car and hauled it away in trucks. They took the rails, too. And that was the end of "Empire Slow & Easy."

A STREETCAR FOR TRAVERSE CITY

It all began back in 1893 with an editorial in the *Grand Traverse Herald*, suggesting that an electric railway be built between Traverse City and Old Mission. Among other things, it said, a railroad would promote the growth of fruit farming by providing fast economic transportation for the produce, hasten the development of the city's suburbs, and stimulate the growth of the summer resort business.

It sounded like a good idea to almost everybody, and in 1897 a corporation was formed for the promotion and development of the Traverse City, Old Mission & Peninsula Railroad. Its president, Lorraine K. Gibbs, had more than civic interest in the project: he as an officer and stockholder in the Queen City Light & Power Company. It was reported that Gibbs had a wealthy friend in New York who would undertake to interest eastern capitalists in the project. Its total cost was projected at $200,000.

Meanwhile, the Corporation raised $20,000 in "good faith money" from local investors—Perry Hannah himself pledged $1,000—and by 1901 it had acquired rights of way from most of the property owners, most of it gratis. Although New York capitalists hadn't exactly stampeded to get a piece of the action, the newspaper reported that a wealthy promoter and contractor from Chicago had arrived in town with his wife to look over the ground and discuss plans and specifications with corporation officials.

The Chicago man stayed all summer at the Park Place Hotel, combining business with pleasure. Upon his departure in the fall he announced that work on the railroad would probably begin in the spring. He was never heard from again. Allegedly he left the hotel with a large unpaid bill for food and lodging.

Nothing daunted, the corporation announced that both Westinghouse and General Electric were interested, and in 1904 the newspaper reported that Westinghouse's chief engineer was in town to survey the ground.

"When this man appears on the scene," the newspaper burbled, "things happen very quickly. His arrival indicates that work on the railroad is about to begin."

As originally conceived, the railroad after leaving the Peninsula would proceed west down Front Street to Union and then make a loop back to Front Street by way of Union, State and Park. Some people objected to the use of State Street, which should be reseved for farmers and their wagons, they said. On the Peninsula, the railroad would hug the eastern shore of the bay.

Somehow the Westinghouse deal fell through, but spokemen for the corporation continued to issue glowing progress reports.

Nevertheless, Henry Hull, president of the Oval Wood Dish Company, was first to throw cold water on the idea. He said it was economically unsound. He had seen the development of successful interurban lines in Ohio, he said, but the population of the Traverse City area was too sparse to support such a railroad.

And so it went, year after year. Work on the railroad was always about to begin, but nothing happened. Not a single shovelful of earth was ever turned. In 1906, investors grew impatient and wanted their money back. All enthusiasm for the project had petered out. Finally, a year or two later, the corporation quietly dissolved, and the baby died a natural death.

RUNAWAY COAL CARS

C ock crow, Wednesday, September 8, 1948. Sunrise at 6:09. A clear brisk late-summer day. At Kingsley, 18 miles south of Traverse City, assistant track foreman Winnie Pierce opens up the Pennsylvania Railroad depot at seven o'clock. He notices that two fully loaded coal cars are standing at the siding a few hundred yards away.

Ten minutes later, two men who work for local coal distributor Leslie Walton drive up in a truck and prepared to set up the conveyor belt for loading the truck. But first they must move the coal cars a few feet so the unloading pockets in the floor of the cars are centered exactly over the elevator openings in the railroad bed. To do this, they must move a weight of some 150 tons. But, no problem. With the use of a pinching bar, it's easier than it sounds. One man climbs up on one of the cars to operate the hand-brake, the other starts pinching the cars forward.

Suddenly the cars begin to roll much faster than they should. The man on the car hollers that the brake won't hold. His partner drops the pinching bar, grabs a loose tie, and shoves it between the wheels. The moving cars brush the cross-tie out of the way and roll ahead, picking up speed. The man on the brake waits as long as he dares, tugging at the wheel, then scrambles down the ladder and jumps for his life.

After a few moments of indecision one of the men runs up the track to the depot. Here he finds Winnie Pierce in the tool shed and explains what has happened. Pierce telephones agent Leo McGee at Traverse City and fills him in. "Great balls of fire!" McGee bellows, and begins to worry. He knows that from Kingsley to Traverse City it's downhill all the way.

Aside from the chance of someone getting hurt at one of the many railroad crossings, there's another major problem. At 7:30 a.m.—just a few minutes before—14 railroad officials from Philadelphia and Chicago have taken off in an inspection car to check the track and bridges between Traverse City and Cadillac. Where is that car now? Will the men in the inspection vehicle see the runaway cars in time to get off the track? Will they all get killed?

All McGee can do now is to alert the police and run down the track and throw a switch, routing the coal cars from the main track to a dead-end siding. And pray.

Back at the depot, section boss Verl McManus hears them coming.

"There was a great roar, like a tornado," McManus says. "How they made it across the river trestle I'll never know. That bridge wasn't strong. It was limited to ten miles an hour. But those cars were going so fast, maybe it didn't have time to collapse."

There is a bunting block at the end of the side-track, but the cars demolish it instantly.

"I stood there and watched," McManus says. "Those cars sailed through the air like a couple of big birds. They smashed into the parking lot at the end of the track and spewed coal all over the place. One car came down piggy-back on the other."

Miraculously, the driver of the inspection car spotted the runaway cars in time to get all of his passengers safely out of the vehicle before the coal cars smashed it into rubble without even a pause.

"It couldn't happen again," says Verl McManus, shaking his head, "not without a bunch of people getting killed. I'll tell you that Old Man up there was watching out for all of us that day."

WERE AUTOMOBILES EVER MANUFACTURED IN TRAVERSE CITY?

Its name was Napoleon, and it originated in 1916 in the little town of Napoleon, Ohio, a few miles southwest of Toledo. Its logo was a rear view of Napoleon Bonaparte himself in full dress uniform, including the familiar bicorn hat.

In 1917, a group of Traverse City people got together at the Chamber of Commerce and decided that an auto plant was just the thing to boost the area's ailing economy, which had been crippled by the loss of Oval Wood Dish Company, the largest industry, to Tupper Lake, New York, in 1916. They had heard good things about the Napoleon, and early that same year they approached the company with an offer of financial assistance if it would relocate to Traverse City.

As it happened, Napoleon had economic problems of its own. Business was good, and it was swamped with orders for the fabulous new machine, but it lacked the necessary capital to increase its production beyond a single unit per day. So both parties were more than willing to cut a deal and it was cinched after only a week or two of negotiations.

A new company was formed with executives from both companies, and it began to raise a start-up capital of $75,000 by selling stock at $10 per share. The price was held purposely low, the company explained, so almost everyone in Traverse City could afford a piece of the action. In full-page advertisements in the *Record-Eagle* people were urged to invest as a kind of patriotic duty, almost on a par with buying World War I Liberty Bonds. Over long lists of happy investors the banner headlines blared: "THESE PEOPLE WANT AN AUTO FACTORY IN TRAVERSE—HOW ABOUT YOU?" and "THESE PEOPLE ARE LUCKY—HOW ABOUT YOU?" and "ONLY SIX

MORE DAYS—EVERYBODY BOOST!" And one day the paper pulled out all stops by printing the following letter:

Nearly everyone in Traverse City has been loyal to our country. We have bought Liberty Bonds and we have aided the Red Cross. Now let us be loyal to our city by buying stock in the new auto company. Don't be a slacker in your home town! I am only a poor widow woman but I love Traverse City and want to see it grow and prosper.

(signed) Mrs. J. Brown

Poor widow woman indeed.

With almost half the start-up money in the bank, Napoleon Motors began operations in November 1917 in the city-owned old Williams Flooring factory on the Boardman River near Boardman Lake—rent free for three years. From the start, the plant produced three Napoleon models: a six-passenger touring car, a smaller 4-passenger car, and a roadster which one newspaper reporter described as "the knobbiest little chummy sport model that has been seen in this city in many a day." The big car was priced at $1,285 and the others at $1,085. Later, a 3/4-ton truck was added; it turned out to be the best seller of all.

The Traverse City factory was basically an assembly plant. It manufactured the car bodies but all other components had to be shipped in by rail. That proved fatal. The Great War had brought about an acute shortage of steel, and from beginning to end Napoleon Motors was plagued by supply shortages, reducing its progress to fits and starts.

In 1918 it produced a disappointing 95 cars and 25 trucks. The next year wasn't much better: 125 cars and 125 trucks. The third year, 1920, looked promising, at least for the first six months, when production rose to five trucks per day. But then the roof fell in. The whole country was gripped in a severe economic recession, and everything for Napoleon went downhill after that. It limped along for two more years and then was forced into bankruptcy, with liabilities of $110,000 and asset of virtually nothing.

A lot of Traverse City people got hurt. The company had sold $650,000 worth of stock to 3,000 investors, mostly local. One of the largest was Julius Steinberg, owner of Steinberg Brothers general store and the Opera House above it. Steinberg was one of Napoleon Motors strongest supporters. When the market started to slip, he offered to redeem $10 Napoleon stock certificates with $10 worth of merchandise. He redeemed so many that he followed Napoleon into bankruptcy in 1926. Other investors included a group of well-known Traverse City sportsmen who papered their hunting and fishing shack on the Boardman River with worthless Napoleon stock certificates.

BIG BOMBER CRASHES NEAR CHARLEVOIX

On the wintry late afternoon of January 7, 1971, the residents of Charlevoix, Michigan, were startled by a huge explosion. This was in Cold War times, and for a few minutes at least, thoughts of Armageddon may have entered their minds. But fears of a nuclear attack, if any, subsided when eyewitness reports began to come in, identifying the source of the explosion. They said that a huge airplane had crashed into the waters of Little Traverse Bay and blew up.

One woman, driving near the crash site, said she saw a light flashing.

"It was frightening," she said. "We didn't know what was happening. It was so bright—just like the sun had been turned on."

Other witnesses said they saw an explosion just before the crash. Still others reported that the plane hit the water, bounced two or three times, then smacked into the icy water in a giant fireball.

The U. S. Coastguard was notified immediately, and help arrived within minutes: two cutters—*Mackinac* and *Sundew*—from the Charlevoix station, two helicopters and a patrol plane from Traverse City. Other watercraft and Air Force and Civil Air planes—

so many they had to be stacked over the area to avoid running into each other—showed up a little later.

Search operations were hampered during the night by blinding snow squalls. Even with the use of powerful flares and search lights, visibility at the crash area was often less than 100 feet. Until morning, when the snow storm eased up a bit, only two life jackets, some debris, and a fuel oil slick—which marked the crash site—had been found.

Next day, more debris, clothing, life preservers, and papers were recovered, but no trace of the members of the crew. It was estimated that the plane went down about 10 miles northeast of Charlevoix, and that the water was about 225 feet deep.

Meanwhile, more information was furnished by headquarters of the Strategic Air Command near Omaha, Nebraska. The missing plane was an unarmed 8-engine B-52 bomber with a crew of nine men, attached to the 99th Bomb Wing at Westover Air Force Base, Mass. It was a routine training flight, dropping electronic bombs which were scored for accuracy on selected targets.

Later, local people told of watching B-52s on similar missions fly into the bay area at low levels from the northwest, passing near the Bayshore radar station, then disappearing over the high ground inland. The simulated bombing range had been in use for several years, they said.

A SAC spokesman reported that radio contact with the big plane had been maintained right up to the last and that there was no hint of trouble.

The search continued for several days without much success. No bodies were ever recovered, and the cause of the crash remains a mystery.

But there's a bronze plaque on a big boulder at the roadside of M-31 near Big Rock Point north of Charlevoix that reads:

IN MEMORIAM

The following B-52 crewmembers gave their lives on a training mission over Lake Michigan: Lt. Col. Wm. B. Lemmon, Lt. Col. John Simoney, Jr., Maj. Gerald W. Black, Maj. Donald P. Rousseau, Capt.

John W. Weaver, Jr., Capt. Joel Hirsch, 1st Lt. Douglas Bachman, 1st Lt. Dennis D. Ferguson, Tech. Sgt. Jerry Achey.

The plaque was placed there by the 99th Bombardment Wing/ SAC, Westover AFB, Mass.

VEGA'S ORDEAL

The terrific gale of November 28, 1905, wasn't the worst of storms on the Great Lakes, but it was bad enough to sink or seriously disable 30 ships and carry 33 people to a watery grave. One was the steamship *Vega*, a bulk carrier out of Ashland, Wisconsin, with a load of iron ore for South Chicago.

Vega departed Ashland in beautiful weather that lasted 24 hours while the ship passed down the length of Lake Superior, through the Soo Locks and the Straits of Mackinac. But then a strong wind driving tattered bits of storm cloud came up suddenly out of the southeast, reaching gale force as the ship passed the Beaver Island archipelago around 10 o'clock Tuesday night. It was accompanied by intense cold, a blinding snowstorm, and brutal waves rolling down almost the full 350-mile length of open Lake Michigan waters.

Unable to make much headway, Captain A. M. Williams ordered helmsman Walter Jantzen to change course from south to a few points southeast. His aim was to seek shelter along the east shore of the Manitou Islands.

Jantzen did his best, struggling for two hours to maintain a steady course against heavy seas, driving snow, and a strong northeast drift, but it was a losing battle. It reached crisis proportions when the seas smashed the pilot house window, dousing the binnacle lights and plunging the compass into darkness.

"The boat was diving and jumping all the time," Jantzen said, "and I couldn't see fifteen yards ahead. The lights were out and I yelled for lights. Two binnacle lamps were brought which lasted about two minutes, the first heavy sea putting them out of business. I then called a second time and the mate arrived and lit them again.

The seas were rushing in over me, and I was drenched and benumbed. The lights went out again, and I managed to light them myself.

"The captain was on watch all night, cool-headed, and he never left the deck except to go below to see how things were down there."

Jantzen said there was no panic, though the crew was stationed at the lifeboats, life preservers on, ready to launch at a moment's notice. It was evident that the ship was laboring and taking on water.

"Suddenly out of the darkness," Jantzen said, "she struck violently on some hidden rock and raised over it, then settled back halfway amidships, the ship immediately breaking in two, the stern on the rocks and the bow well to forward. Captain Williams immediately gave orders for all to go forward and await daylight."

Jantzen said they were all drenched, cold, and unprotected, but the day broke, they saw North Fox Island in the darkness and realized that the land ahead, about a half mile away, was the northwest point of South Fox Island. The *Vega* now lay on the rocky bottom in about twenty feet of water, with the bow headed south and the broken stern to the southeast. The foundering occurred at 4:30 a.m. All together, the captain and crew remained on the wreck for eight hours before the storm subsided enough for them to launch the lifeboats. They lost the first one but managed to launch the second, which carried five men to South Fox Island beach. Several Indians had gathered there and built a huge bonfire in readiness for them.

The Indians, Lewis Ance and his family, and his son-in-law and family, were the only inhabitants of the island. They returned to the wreck in the lifeboat and brought off the remainder of the crew, making three trips before all were safely landed. The crew spent Tuesday and Wednesday on the island and left Thursday noon for Northport in the Indian boats after a Thanksgiving dinner with their rescuers. The Captain and the nineteen members of the crew couldn't say enough in praise of the Indians' kindness and help.

Vega's skipper, A. M. Williams, was apparently one of those strong, silent, imperturbable men like Captain McWhirr of the *Nan-Shan* in Joseph Conrad's great story *Typhoon*.

"Yes, we had our troubles out there," he admitted to reporters in what may have been the understatement of the year.

TWO MISHAPS ON THE GR&I

The Grand Rapids & Indiana Railroad had its share of wrecks and mishaps over the years. But it should be pointed out that its safety record, like that of most railroads, was remarkably good.

One of the most amusing accidents happened in the summer of 1890. A Reed City man named Belknap was returning home late one night on the railroad after a business trip in the north. Hearing the conductor call out "Reed City", he picked up his valise and went to the door. When the train came to a stop, he descended the steps in the dark, grip in hand, and plunged 12 feet into the Hersey River.

The train had stopped to take on water at a tank just north of town, leaving the passenger cars on a bridge over the river. Belknap fished himself out of the water, suffering only the loss of his baggage and dignity, but a newspaper story the next day called him the "angriest passenger on the Grand Rapids & Indiana."

Another mishap that could have had serious consequences, but didn't, took place on Saturday afternoon, February 14, 1903. Between 4:30 and 5 o'clock locomotive engineer Dailey was switching freight cars in the yard at Kingsley when one of them broke loose and headed down the track toward Mayfield. Brakeman Dooley was up on the car struggling with the hand brake, and he called out that it wasn't holding. He was told to stay there.

Engineer Dailey threw the six cars ahead of him onto a side track and with Conductor Phil Griffin riding on a pilot (a footboard at the front end of the engine), swung the engine onto the main line in hot pursuit. On the stretch to Mayfield they caught sight of the runaway car as it disappeared around a curve after barreling through the village like an express train.

What worried the men most was that the 4:30 p.m. passenger train had already left the Traverse City depot, and there was no way they could get in touch with the crew. Railroad men had long believed that the grade between Kingsley and the Boardman River was so steep that a runaway car would run all the way to Traverse City without a stop.

Fortunately, thanks to Brakeman Dooley, whose valiant efforts at the hand brake had slowed the car at least a little, and because the grade in the river valley was considerably less steep than assumed, the engine caught up with the freight car between Mitchell Junction and Sleights. Conductor Griffin jumped down and made a coupling on the run. Dooley dropped off to flag down the passenger train. And Dailey towed the car back to Kingsley, followed a few minutes later by the passenger train.

Later it was learned that the passenger train had stopped at Sleights to unload several passengers. Otherwise, said the railroad men, a serious wreck could hardly have been avoided.

THE STORY OF THE TCL&M

Envy was one reason for building the Traverse City, Leelanau & Manistique Railroad. The Grand Rapids & Indiana Railroad was envious of its rivals: the Ann Arbor, Pere Marquette, and Grand Trunk railroads. All had cross-lake ferries, and GR&I wanted one, too.

Its original plan was to establish a carferry line between Traverse City and Manistique. But that was scrubbed when somebody pointed out that Grand Traverse Bay was usually ice-bound for two or three months of the year. Finally it was decided to build the ferry slip at Northport and a railroad to it from Traverse City.

Construction of the new railroad began in 1902. Most of the grading was done by Leelanau County farmers with teams of horses. Originally, the plan was to lay the tracks parallel to the Manistee & Northeastern's track from Traverse City to Hatches Crossing—a distance of about 5.5 miles—but later it was judged more practical to rent the use of M&NE tracks over that distance.

Meanwhile, work on the ferry slip at Northport was in progress, and a carferry was under construction at Cleveland, Ohio, at a cost of $400,000. Named Manistique & Northern No. 1, she was a steel ship of about 3,000 gross tons and 338 feet in length. With her four railroad tracks she could accommodate 30 railroad cars. A second ship was planned but never built.

Construction on the TCL&M was completed in May 1903, and the first train arrived at Northport on June 1. It was welcomed by church bells, a brass band, and crowds of people dancing in the streets. "Out of the woods—out of the woods at last!" proclaimed one of the banners. The 29-mile run—with stops at Hatches Crossing, Suttons Bay, and Omena—took about two hours. The schedule changed somewhat over the years and the seasons, but at least one passenger train ran every day except Sunday.

Ferry service to Manistique opened in October 1903, but it ran into trouble almost from the start. Financial problems, disappointing freight loadings, and bad weather hampered its fitful service, and it went out of business in 1908. The ferry boat was sold to the Pere Marquette for service from Grand Haven to Milwaukee. She served there until 1929, when she was lost with all hands near Milwaukee in the great storm of October 22. It was the worst disaster ever to befall a Great Lakes ferry.

The TCL&M had a much longer life. But profit margins were thin after loss of the ferry, and the GR&I sold it to a group of Suttons Bay businessmen in 1919. Passenger service continued until 1948, and the last freight train to Suttons Bay ran in 1979, the Suttons Bay-Northport branch having been abandoned in the 1960s. After an unsuccessful attempt to establish an excursion train from Traverse City to Suttons Bay in the early 1990s, the rails and ties were taken up, and the roadbed became the Leelanau Trail.

Old-timers in Leelanau County look back on the TCL&M with nostalgia. It played an important part in their lives. It was fast, dependable, and pleasant, and it beat a trip to town in a horse and buggy all hollow.

MAURICE HULETT: ENGINE MAN

Hardly anybody these days has a good word for the internal combustion engine—so Maurice Hulett of Kingsley was something of a rarity. He loved gasoline engines.

That is to say, he loved OLD gas engines—the old fashioned stationary kind with the big flywheel and the magneto or make-and-break coil, the kind that grandpa used, years ago, to buzz up firewood back of the barn. The kind that goes chug-pocka-pocka chug-pocka-pocka. Or something like that.

Hulett started collecting gas engines fifty or sixty years ago. Over the years he collected more than a hundred of them: engines of all sizes, shapes, and descriptions. They were lined up on his farm just south of Kinglsey, and they occupied a good-sized chunk of land, for, as Hulett said, with a chuckle, "It isn't like collecting stamps or old coins. For this kind of hobby you need plenty of room."

How did he get interested in old gas engines?

"Well, it goes back a long way," Hulett said, a big affable man with friendly blue eyes and a quiet sense of humor. "When I was a kid, there was a man named Jim Smith, who owned a blacksmith shop down the road from here. Besides blacksmithing he ground corn for the farmers and made lath and other things. He used his big gas engine to operate his machinery, and that old engine used to wake me up every morning. After breakfast I'd run down to old man Smith's and watch his engine running for hours at a time."

"It fascinated me. All kids in those days were fascinated by gasoline engines, which were fairly new then, everything before that being operated with steam. I wasn't interested in Smith's other machinery. I just loved to watch that big gas engine."

"Then, during school days it was my alarm clock. When I heard Jim Smith's engine start up, I knew it was time to get up…. The sound of that big engine sorta got in my blood, I guess. It stayed with me, and that's one reason I started collecting old gas engines."

Hulett picked up engines all over this part of the country—from farmers, junk dealers, old mills—wherever he could find them. Most of them had a story to tell, and Hulett knew a lot about their history. He also knew the makes and models and the dates of manufacture, even though many of the name plates were missing.

His largest engine, a monster weighing almost three tons, came from Omena. It was owned by a man named John Bauer, who operated a fishbox factory there years ago. One of his smallest engines was used to power an aboriginal lawn mower. In the days before wide-spread availability of electricity, stationary gas engines were used for many purposes on the farm: buzzing wood, milking cows, separating cream, and pumping water.

"Some collectors are perfectionists," Hulett said. "They will dismantle an old engine down to the last nut and bolt and then replace any part that's even a little bit defective. I'm not that particular. I clean them up with a wire brush, steel wool and a solvent—and plenty of elbow grease—and get them in good running order." Although Hulett keeps his collection out under the open sky, most of them will bang right off with a turn or two of the crank.

"More and more people are getting interested in old engines and other old farm machinery," Hulett said. "We have our own national magazine, the Gas Engine, published in Pennsylvania."

Hulett was a mail carrier in Kingsley for 30 years and an employee at the State Hospital in Traverse City for 18.

"I guess it's a kind of nostalgia. In troubled times, people are turning to the old things. But it isn't just the older folks—even the kids are interested." He grinned. "Of course the kids like those souped-up gas-gulping auto engines, too."

But with Hulett of Kingsley, hobbyist extraordinary, it was no contest. He preferred the old-fashioned kind, the stationary engine with the big flywheel, the kind—you know—that goes chug-pocketa-pocketa, chug-pocketa-pocketa. Or something like that.

TRAGEDY AT SEA

On Thursday morning, June 22, 1933, a Stinson monoplane with pontoon landing gear took off from Traverse City carrying four people bound for Milwaukee. They never got there.

They were Charles E. Rennie, Jr., vice-president of the Rennie Oil Company, and his wife Margaret; her brother James "Timber" Gillette, owner and pilot of the plane; and Peter Keller, mechanic. The purpose of the trip was to obtain a harbor permit to build a dock on Grand Traverse Bay for the Rennie Oil Company's new storage plant at Greilickville. Ben Samuelson, contractor, had been invited to make the trip but at the last moment gave up his seat to Mrs. Rennie.

Sometime between 9 and 10 o'clock the plane was sighted over Frankfort and Elberta and then striking out over Lake Michigan south of the Wabash Radio Corporation's land station at Elberta. Curiously and fatefully, the plane carried no radio equipment, no means of summoning help.

Almost immediately the plane struck a thick fog bank, and Gillette decided to land on the water and taxi back to shore. That was a bad mistake. What he should have done was make a 180-degree turn and put the plane down nearer the shore, where visibility was much better. Instead, because of the fog, he put the plane in a dive so steep that the altimeter couldn't keep up with it, and he hit the water so hard that the pontoons were crushed. They were about 15 miles southwest of Frankfort when it happened.

In the short time that the plane remained afloat the men managed to strip the gas tank from one of the wings and fashion a crude raft four feet square and six inches thick. On top of it they tied a large cushion from the plane. Then, as the plane sank, they took to the water. After boosting Mrs. Rennie up on the float, they held on to one side of it and tried to propel it toward shore with a swimmer's kick but made little progress. Slowly, with a mild southern breeze, they drifted north, talking, singing, and praying, trying to encourage each other.

Timber Gillette said to his sister, "I got you into this and I will get you out."

Throughout the long day, at least seven ships passed by without spotting them in the fog.

That night Peter Keller began talking in a strange manner, and despite the others' efforts, he slipped away. Next to go was Gillette; he lapsed into a coma and sank. Next morning, totally exhausted and numb, Charles Rennie clambered up on the raft beside his wife but soon began to lose consciousness.

"Please don't go, Chick," his wife begged. "I'm all right," he said, but slipped off the float and was gone. Hours before, he had given his wife his wristwatch, a family heirloom. It had been presented by the city to his grandfather, John "Black Jack" Rennie, upon his appointment as Chief of Police in 1894.

Mrs. Rennie, after her terrible ordeal of 34 hours adrift—15 of them all alone—was rescued late Friday afternoon by a passing Ann Arbor line carferry out of Frankfort bound for Kewaunee, Wisconsin. One of the officers spotted the float and heard her cries. She was taken on board and put to bed, attended by the ship's doctor and a matron. Surprisingly, she suffered no serious injury and was almost fully recovered when the boat returned to Frankfort the next day.

"The only thing that gave me strength to fight on was that the men made me comfortable on the raft," she said. "Otherwise, I know I wouldn't have lasted long in the water."

HIGH BRIDGE OVER THE MANISTEE RIVER

On January 28, 1872, the *Grand Traverse Herald* ran a story about the arrival of Traverse City's first railroad, the Grand Rapids & Indiana. The story included mention of another railroad that also seemed headed for Traverse City at the time:

The Lakeshore Railroad will soon be completed to Pentwater, and probably before the close of 1873 will reach Manistee. What the northern terminus will be is at present unknown. Our friends at Frankfort, Glen Arbor, Leland, and other places along the lake, expect it to follow the shore. If it does, all right; we will rejoice with the people who win; but we, of Traverse City, expect it to come here by a nearly direct route from Manistee. Our faith is very strong, and we hope for its coming.

Their faith was eventually confirmed, but they had to wait a long time. It was 18 years before the railroad reached Traverse City, and by that time it had acquired a different name.

The Michigan Lake Shore never did reach Manistee; it got no farther north than Pentwater. Then came the Panic of 1873. It halted virtually all railroad construction during the 1870s, and brought many railroads to the verge of bankruptcy.

In 1881 the Lake Shore merged with three smaller lines to form Chicago & West Michigan Railroad Company; one of those smaller lines was operating between Grand Rapids and White Cloud. The C&WM completed an extension of this line to Baldwin in 1883, and began to build slowly on to the north, reaching the Manistee River just north of Wellston in 1887. Here it faced a problem of considerable magnitude.

The C&WM's High Bridge over the Manistee was an engineering marvel. The route surveyed for the river crossing followed a line of glacial hills lying roughly north and south. The river had cut a broad valley through them, leaving high sandy bluffs on both sides. The High Bridge spanned a gap of 1,196 feet and stood 87 feet above the river's high water mark. It was built of heavy timbers that rested on 58 stone and concrete piers. It was rebuilt of steel in 1911.

One of the thrills of riding the train from Traverse City to Chicago in the late 1940s and the 1950s (the trip took nearly 15 hours) was crossing the High Bridge. By that time it was so shaky that the engineer had to slow down to five miles per hour. But the eeriest part of it was looking down at the river 87 feet below. You couldn't see any part of the bridge at that perspective, and it seemed as though the train were suspended in thin air.

The bridge was finally dismantled in 1955.

SHIPS OF HANNAH, LAY & COMPANY

The first Hannah, Lay & Company sailing ship was the brig *J. Y. Scammon*. She was wrecked in the Manitou Passage in 1854, her first year of service.

A year earlier, the company had purchased the *Telegraph*, a two-masted schooner of 267 tons, 117 feet long by 26 feet wide. In 1856, she was sold to her master, Captain Ira Harrison, and chartered to the company. She carried lumber from the Traverse City sawmill to Chicago at least until 1860, when on April 12 she was the first arrival of the season at Traverse City, with Perry Hannah himself on board.

The first Hannah, Lay steamship was the propeller *Allegheny*. She was built at Milwaukee in 1854 for the American Transportation Company at a cost of $46,500. That company failed in 1858, and she was bought by Hannah, Lay in 1860 at the bargain price of $14,000. In April of that year she opened a regular run of freight and passengers between Traverse City and Chicago. On her first voyage she carried 300,000 feet of timber and several passengers, including Morgan Bates, editor and publisher of the *Grand Traverse Herald*.

Allegheny's doughty Captain C. H. Boynton became seriously ill in 1866 and was replaced for the 1867 season by Captain George Baldwin. She continued in service for four more years, making weekly round trips to Chicago, and sometimes to Port Huron and Detroit. During her first six years she had kept Traverse City informed on the course of the Civil War by picking up the latest newspapers at Chicago and Detroit. Over the years she carried 72 million board feet of lumber for Hannah, Lay & Company, and 18 million shingles.

Many a Traverse citizen brushed away a tear when it was announced in the *Grand Traverse Herald*, in November of 1870, that she had been sold and would be converted into a barge for service on Lake St. Clair. "Goodbye, *Allegheny*," wrote the Herald's editor D. C. Leach.

To replace the *Allegheny* the company commissioned Quale & Martin of Cleveland to build an elegant steamer, *City of Traverse* in 1870 at a cost of $85,000. She was 225 feet long and 32 feet wide, with accommodations for 75 passengers and 640,000 board feet of lumber, three times as much as the *Allegheny*. On her arrival at Traverse City on May 4, 1871, she was greeted by a large crowd of people, who went aboard to admire such splendid furnishings as her Brussels carpeting and black walnut furniture. Her Captain was George Baldwin, recent skipper of the *Allegheny*, and her clerk and steward was Stephen E. Wait, one of Traverse City's earliest pioneers.

She began her weekly run to Chicago a few days later. During the first year of service she made 23 round trips to Chicago, carrying 12,639,950 feet of lumber. Altogether she brought to Traverse City 60,000 bushels of grain and carried 1,040 passengers.

City of Traverse served the company until 1887 (when Hannah, Lay went out of the lumber business) and was sold to the Graham and Morton Line for use between Chicago and Lake Superior ports.

Her end was ignominious. After passing through several other owners, she came under the control of a Chicago gang syndicate and used as a gambling ship offshore. Finally, she was left to disintegrate in the mud at Benton Harbor. A Chicago newspaper on September 28, 1907, printed her epitaph:

> *Drawn up at the end of the canal at Benton Harbor, Michigan, its nose poking into the mud, her bow half concealed by the heavy growth of weeds on either side of the channel, lies the good ship City of Traverse . . . .*

For two and a half years she was the principal actor in an extraordinary attempt on the part of Chicago gangsters by means of modern science. The big ship was rigged as a floating poolroom, equipped with a wireless telegraphic outfit and commissioned as a means of transmitting race track results regardless of the police.

A RAILROAD SIDING CALLED TUNK

Only a few people remember Tunk.

One of them is Ray Boyd, who grew up on a farm in eastern Grand Traverse County near Mabel. Its eighty acres are bisected north and south by Baggs Road and transected east and west by the Pere Marquette Railroad. Ray not only remembers Tunk; he also knows how it got its name.

Tunk was a railroad siding on the PM RR. It lay in the middle of the Boyd farm about a quarter of the mile west of the Baggs Road crossing. It consisted of a side track, a hand-operated switch, a small shed for railroad tools and a handcar, and, really, that's about all. Ray remembers that as a boy he would watch the "stone trains" pass by, as many as two or three every day.

In the early 1900s, the "stone trains" hauled large quantities of limestone rock from the quarry at Petoskey. The stone went to southern Michigan lakeside cities for use in building breakwaters, cribs, and piers. Some of it went to the big iron furnace in Muskegon— Campbell, Wyatt & Cannon—for use in smelting iron.

It wasn't unusual, Ray says, to see the southbound trains with as many as a hundred cars filled with limestone hauled by as many as three engines, two pulling and one pushing. But from the east end of Skegemog Lake the trains had to climb a fairly steep grade to Barker Creek and beyond. There was no way that even three engines could haul more than thirty or forty limestone-laden cars up that steep slope. So the crew would break down the cars into strings, and the engines would haul up one string at a time, deposit it on the side-track, and then go back for another. In railroad lingo that was called "doubling the hill."

Ray says that even then the loads were so heavy that the engines would be chattering with the strain as they went up the hill. To the farm people nearby it sounded like "tunk—tunk—tunk." And that, he says, is how Tunk got its name.

Nothing is left of Tunk today. The rails and ties on this stretch of the Pere Marquette were taken up years ago. Long before that, the railroad men cut a deep ditch on each side of the main track, obscuring the side track. Like so many places where the railroad went—stations, switchyards, whistle stops, and sidings—Tunk now is just a memory.

SHADOWS BEFORE

Six men died in the worst train wreck in Traverse City history because five men had a lapse of memory. Of those five, three paid the extreme penalty. It happened on Wednesday, August

20, 1919. Frank W. Cushman, a postal clerk on the passenger train, who died instantly, is said to have had a warning.

Pere Marquette Railroad's passenger train No. 6, southbound, left Union Street station at 11:20 that morning. Fletcher Gage, formerly of Traverse City but now residing in Grand Rapids, was hauling a light load of passengers. His fireman was Earl Beeman, also from Grand Rapids.

No. 6 passed the Boardman yards south of town at 11:32, exactly on time. It proceeded south along the Boardman River toward Beitner, gradually picking up the necessary speed to climb Grawn Hill, after making the big curve to the west just below Beitner.

At 11:31, precisely one minute before the passenger train passed Boardman, extra freight train No. 362, from Grand Rapids, was at Grawn, traveling slowly. The telegraph operator there expected the freight to stop and back into a siding, clearing the tracks for No. 6. Instead it kept on going, picking up speed as it approached the steep grade into the river valley. From that time on, both trains were in deadly peril.

Freight 362 had a medium weight load, a string of coal cars. Its crew of five included engineer Earl G. Eighmy, conductor Fred S. Neubecker, fireman Guy L. Shenneman, and brakemen F. J. David and Roy Peets, all of Grand Rapids. All were experienced railroad men. Engineer Eighmy had a spotless record of 15 years with the railroad.

Suddenly a thought flashed through his mind: The southbound passenger train. He had forgotten the passenger train! So, apparently, had the rest of the crew! A few seconds later, before he had time to sound a warning, there was a terrific crash as the two engines hit head on.

According to witnesses, the two engines were thrown at least 40 feet into the air. Telescoped by the tenders into the cabs, they came down one on top of the other, a smoking, seething mass of twisted steel. So great was the impact that one 400 pound piece of the frame was hurled 200 feet to the bank of the Boardman River. There was no explosion because the boilers of both engines remained intact, but one of the steam pipes snapped, letting loose a three-inch jet of steam with a screaming howl that could be heard for miles.

Strangely enough, there was no great jar throughout the length of the passenger cars, which remained on the tracks. Few of the passengers suffered more than minor cut and bruises. The absence of casualties among the passengers was attributed to the recent replacement of the wooden cars with steel coaches.

But for the train crews it was a different story. The bodies of six of them were buried somewhere in that mess of twisted steel, and the grim task of finding them went forward all afternoon and into the night. A wrecking crane and crew reached the scene by early afternoon and began clearing away the debris.

Four of the bodies were recovered that afternoon, crushed beyond recognition. Fletcher Gage was found beneath the engine tender. Frank Cushman of Petoskey was found beneath the freight engine, as was the body of freight brakeman F. J. Davis. Earl Beeman, the passenger train fireman, was still alive when pulled from the wreckage, but died later that afternoon. The bodies of Earl Eighmy, the freight engineer, and his fireman Guy Shenneman, were not found until late Friday afternoon after tons of coal, twisted metal, and other debris had been removed from the right of way.

Freight conductor Fred S. Neubecker and brakeman Roy Peets told virtually the same story in their testimony before a coroner's jury. Until Neubecker's flash of memory just before the crash, all of the crew had forgotten the passenger train.

"I tell you, we simply forgot about it," said Conductor Neubecker with tears running down his cheeks. He reached into his pocket and pulled out some papers. "Here's our time-table and here is my watch. It was our business to keep out of the way of the passenger train, and we failed. It's the first thing I've had against me in 28 years of service on the railroad."

Frank W. Cushman, the mail clerk who was killed instantly, made a curious remark to his landlady as he left his rooming house at 61-1/2 Lagrave Aveune in Grand Rapids for his last trip north.

"Goodbye," he said. "My home is in heaven."

No one afterward could figure out what he meant.

PASSENGER BOATS ON LAKE LEELANAU

More like a river than a lake, Lake Leelanau (originally called Carp Lake) is about fifteen miles long and on the average scarcely more than half a mile wide. From north to south it neatly bisects the eastern half of the Leelanau County peninsula, and the only bridge across it is over the narrows at the village of Lake Leelanau (originally called Provemont). In the early days, it provided a convenient short-cut waterway from Leland in the north to Fouch in the south—only seven miles from Traverse City—saving nearly half the distance by road.

The first commercial passenger boat on Lake Leelanau was the little steamer *Sally*. She began operations in the spring of 1892 under her master, Morgan Cummings, who had been employed at the Leland Iron Company. She made one trip daily between Leland and Fouch, with stops at Provemont and Bingham Landing. At Fouch she made connection with the newly arrived Manistee & Northeastern Railroad. Leelanau County people could catch the *Sally* and meet the M&NE in the morning, spend seven hours in Traverse City, and take the railroad and the boat homeward in the late afternoon. *Sally* was also available for charter fishing trips on the lake.

About 1894, another small steamer, *Tiger*, under Captain John Hartung, replaced *Sally*, and operated on the same schedule.

In 1900, Louis Mosier, owner of Mosier's mill, built the steam propeller *Leelanau* with the help of his two sons, Leo and Joe. Designed by Louis Hockstead of Bingham, she was 68 feet ten inches long and 15 feet abeam. She was built of heavy tamarack planking and a 6-inch by 6-inch rock elm frame. Her ribs were cooked in open-air kettles and bent to shape by hand. Her practically new engine and boiler were taken from the steamer *Ransom*, which had been brought from Buffalo a year or two previously by Louis Mosier and Morgan Cummings. In competition with the *Tiger*, she began operations on Lake Leelanau in 1901.

An intense rivalry between the two boats led to a price war, which, over the next couple of years, reduced the round-trip fare from Leland to Fouch from $1.50 to $1.00 and then to 75 cents. The time card for both vessels called for two round trips daily, one in the morning and one in the afternoon, with stops at Provemont, Fountain Point, Horton's, Bingham Landing, and Nolan's.

The *Leelanau* was successful in driving the older *Tiger* off the lake, but on August 16, 1908 she met with tragedy. Off Bingham Landing her vertical boiler blew up with a terrific roar. The blast threw passenger Mrs. Isabelle LaBonte overboard, and her body wasn't found until five days later. It was ironic that John Hartung, former skipper of the *Tiger* (he had sold the *Tiger* to Bernie Pickard for use as a tug on Lake Michigan) was at the wheel of the *Leelanau* when the explosion occurred. He was severely scalded by steam and boiling water and died a few days later at Munson Hospital.

Interviewed by an *Evening Record* reporter, owner Charles Mosier said that he believed a flaw in the dome of the boiler caused the explosion. Somewhat defensively he added, "Does anyone think that if I imagined there was a chance of the boiler going up that I would sit, day after day, right above it for hours at a time? I think too much of my wife and babies for anything like that."

After lying at Bingham Landing for some time, the *Leelanau* was sold to John VerSnyder. He outfitted her with a new engine and boiler and continued to operate on Lake Leelanau until 1929, when ill health forced him to retire. It is said that VerSnyder beached the boat near his home, raked the coals out from under her boiler, and never set foot on her again.

The *Leelanau* was left to disintegrate slowly in the mud. Her boiler is said to have been taken to Traverse City for use by the Grand Traverse Metal Casket Company. Some of the timber from her hull and pilothouse reportedly went into a house on the Wilburt Gauthier farm three miles south of the village of Lake Leelanau.

Another small steamboat, *Carrie Palmer*, made regular trips between Leland and Provemont for a season or two beginning in 1909. She was owned and skippered by Charles Mosier.

CHERRIES AND THE FESTIVAL

CHERRY FESTIVAL 1930

President Herbert Hoover was a sourpuss, but New York Mayor Jimmy Walker was full of his usual graciousness and charm. That's how it was during Cherry Queen Signe Holmer's three-day airplane trip to Washington and New York in June 1930.

Michigan Senator Arthur Vandenberg had a hard time persuading Hoover to attend the ceremony, but the President finally accepted the big cherry pie from the Queen. Then, in an almost audible aside to one of his aides, "Give it to the poor," he said. Hoover wasn't usually so grumpy but the Great Depression was already getting him down.

Jimmy Walker's pie got smashed in a rough landing at Roosevelt Airport. Nevertheless, he greeted her with a warm smile and said he regretted the loss of the pie. Queen Signe's promotional trip, the first of its kind, established a tradition that has lasted to this day, helping to put canned cherries in the nation's cupboards and Traverse City on the map.

Blonde and beautiful, Signe Holmer, 18, of Manistee, had been chosen queen from a field of 15 candidates at the Lyric Theater on June 9, 1930.

The 1929 festival had been so successful that General Chairman Larry Larsen (local Bell Telephone manager) and his committee decided to make the 1930 festival a three-day affair— Wednesday, Thursday, and Friday.

New among the mix of features was the air show put on by three National Guard airplanes from Selfridge Field, including parachute jumps at Ransom Field south of town. On Thursday morning at 10, Queen Signe opened the throttle on the "Cherryland Special", an 18-car train-load of cherries, the first of the season. The ceremony took place at the Pere Marquette siding on Union Street; former Governor Chase Osborn was the speaker.

"Eating cherries," he said with arguable logic, "is going to make for a stronger mankind." Pathe Newsreel filmed the Queen and her court as they packed boxes of cherries for President Herbert Hoover, Mayor Jimmy Walker, and Vice President Rufus Dawes.

Among the 50 floats in Friday's Grand Floral Parade, Peninsula took first prize and Traverse City Lumber Company second. The parade was led by Marshall Josephine Kehoe on horseback, accompanied by Mrs. M. Holdsworth, Fern Blanchard, and Elizabeth Vaughn. It marched through town from Garfield to Elmwood.

In other events, Jack Wood, driving his "Detroit Kid", nosed out Traverse City's Ben Samuelson for first place in the 20-mile Ford Island Marathon motorboat race; the winning time was 40 minutes, 40 seconds. And the famous Jean Goldkette and his orchestra furnished the music for the Governor's Ball at the Traverse City Country Club on Friday night.

NATIONAL CHERRY FESTIVAL 1933

Eleanor Roosevelt was invited to crown the Cherry Queen, but she couldn't make it, so Michigan Senator Arthur Vandenberg substituted for the First Lady at the ceremony on Thursday, July 20, 1933, the second day of the three-day festival.

That job traditionally belonged to Michigan's Governor, but newly elected Democrat William A. Comstock had made a campaign promise not to indulge in crowning festival queens. He was nevertheless invited to attend the festival, and on Thursday night, at the Governor's Ball, he made a full apology: "I had no conception of the magnitude nor importance and significance of the National Cherry Festival until I viewed the one now under way," he said.

He was forgiven.

Later that night, a hatless and coatless man rapped at one of the cottage doors of the Traverse City State Hospital (commonly known as The Asylum) and asked for the Governor.

"Oh, yes," the matron told him soothingly. "We have governors, senators, presidents, and kings here."

It took some time for Ferris Fitch, secretary to Governor Comstock, to convince her that he was not seeking admission but actually looking for the Governor. She directed him to the main office where his boss was attending a meeting of the hospital's Board of Directors. Fitch had driven to Traverse City from Lansing that evening with some legislative bills for the Governor to sign.

Morella Oldham of Charlevoix was chosen Cherry Queen from a slate of eight candidates, and Ruth Knapp of Traverse City was first runner-up and thus became Maid of Honor. Morella was the daughter of an English couple, who had named her, appropriately enough, after a kind of cherry grown back home in England, Morella cherries.

Rain threatened the Grand Floral Parade but again the festival's luck with the weather held good. It followed a new route that year. Beginning at the intersection of Front and Railroad, it went west to Wadsworth, then south to Seventh and east to Union Street. Then it swung north to State and east past the judges' stand at the Park Place Hotel to Wellington Street, where it disbanded.

Leading the parade was Grand Marshall Frederica Galbraith of Northport Point and Asheville, North Carolina. She was accompanied by five other girls on horseback and three moppets on black ponies. Among the outstanding marching bands were the Manistee Iron Works' 30 pieces in red, green and white; the Beulah-Benzonia Band; the 30-piece Charlevoix Band; and the Traverse City High School Band in traditional black and gold, under the direction of Dewey Kalember.

Perhaps the most popular float was the Manistee Brewing Company's floating beer garden that dispensed free beer along the line of march in celebration of the end of Prohibition. There were many partakers.

1937 CHERRY QUEEN GETS
BACK AT DIZZY DEAN

Irrepressible Dizzy Dean stuck his finger in the President's cherry pie. He licked his finger and smacked his lips. "Um, that's good," he said. Then he wiped his finger dry on the Cherry Queen's white glove. That happened in Pittsburg on July 6, 1937. The Queen, Eliene Lyon of Old Mission, was not amused.

Next day she delivered the pie to President Franklin Roosevelt at the White House. After surveying her and the two-foot-diameter pie, the President said he was glad to see the National Cherry Festival was maintaining its high standards all around. They chatted for a while about cherries and fishing.

Queen Eliene got back at Dizzy Dean that afternoon at the All-Star baseball game at Griffith Stadium. She cheered ardently for the American League as it trounced Dizzy Dean and the National League All-Stars by a score of 8 to 3. Baseball fans will remember that this was the game where Dizzy broke his toe on a line drive from Earl Averill, an injury that would soon put an end to the great pitcher's career.

The Queen also paid a call on Ambassador Hirosi Saito at the Japanese Embassy. He promised to attend the National Cherry Festival that year, and he was as good as his word. He arrived in Traverse City on the evening of July 15, final day of the three-day festival, just in time to place the jeweled crown on brunette Eliene's pretty head. The Ambassador made a little speech, pledging Japan's undying friendship with the American people. The ceremony took place on the beautifully decorated platform on the shores of Grand Traverse Bay.

From there the royal party and the Ambassador had to hurry across town to open the Queen's Ball at the Country Club, where they led the Grand March. The Club's ballroom was decorated with the red and white national colors of Japan. More than 300 couples from all over the resort region attended the Ball, Maurie Sherman's orchestra furnishing the music. Festoons of Japanese lanterns hung about the grounds.

The Grand Floral Parade on Friday was judged the best ever, and the crowd was estimated at 100,000. There were 45 floats and 11 marching bands. The National Forest Service's float showing a coon hunter and other recreational activities of Michigan's forests would have taken first prize, but the department made it clear that its participation in the Parade was not competitive.

Prince and Princess at the Juvenile Parade on Thursday afternoon were Richard Solomonson and Yvonne Coutourier. Leo P. Kalahar served once more as general chairman of the festival.

1941 CHERRY FESTIVAL

Joe Louis, the Brown Bomber, was the biggest attraction at the 1941 Cherry Festival, July 16, 17, 18. He refereed several of the Golden Gloves boxing matches at the Fairgrounds on Friday evening, July 18. Louis in 1941 was at the peak of his career, having kayoed James Braddock for the heavyweight title in 1937 and cold-cocked Germany's Max Schmeling in the first round of their re-match in 1938. Local boy Alva Carnahan won his Golden Gloves bout with Glen McCoy of Ludington in the lightweight division.

Continuing the precedent set in 1940, when an outsider had won the Queen's crown, Senorita Christine Michels of Chile was chosen Queen. Her father was Chilean ambassador to the U. S. and a good friend of Senator Arthur Vandenberg, who had something to do with the selection, it was said.

Not everyone was pleased. The *Lansing State Journal* grumbled that the choice was ill-advised, since Chile was reported to be friendly with Nazi Germany. But the Ambassador said that he didn't like dictators, and everything came out all right at the end, since Queen Christine won the hearts of all her subjects with her charm and beauty.

The Festival opened on Wednesday with the arrival of Queen Christine aboard the cutter *Hollywood*. It was followed by a reception in her honor at the Fairgrounds, where the Queen received her royal diadem from Governor Murray VanWagoner. Francis Kildee and Shelley England served as Prince and Princess.

The rain came down in sheets next morning, and the Grand Floral Parade was postponed for an hour. It finally got started at 2 p.m., and except for a few sprinkles which went almost unnoticed, the rain held off until the last float had passed by.

Fireworks over the bay and the Mummer Parade—with radio personality Smilin' Ed McConnell as Mummers King—provided the grand finale.

The country was now at war in everything but name. War was declared against Japan and Germany in December 1941; and six long years would pass before another Cherry Festival would take place.